MW01259297

Interactive Notetaking

for Content-Area Literacy

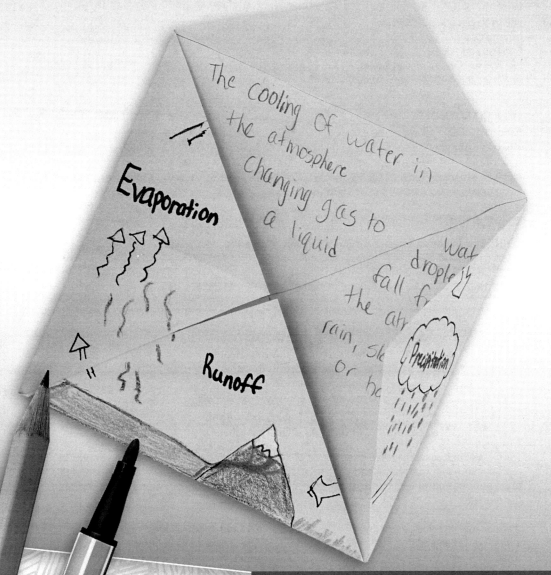

Judith Goodman, M.A.Ed.

Publishing Credits

Corinne Burton, M.A.Ed., *Publisher*
Conni Medina, M.A.Ed., *Managing Editor*
Emily R. Smith, M.A.Ed., *Content Director*
Veronique Bos, *Creative Director*
Shaun N. Bernadou, *Art Director*
Lynette Ordoñez, *Editor*
Dana Strong, *Editor*
Lee Aucoin, *Senior Graphic Designer*
Stephanie Bernard, *Associate Editor*

Image Credits

front cover Walter Mladina; p.38 Library of Congress [LC-DIG-ggbain-38336]; p.84 (top right) Kenneth Libbrecht/Science Source; p.103 Library of Congress [LC-DIG-det-4a26004]; p.111 (top) Drop of Light/Shutterstock; p.123 Library of Congress [LC_USZC4_2634]; p.131 National Archives and Records Administration [306-PS-50-7551]; p.132 Science History Images/Alamy Stock Photo; all other images from iStock and/or Shutterstock.

Standards

© 2014 Mid-continent Research for Education and Learning
© Copyright 2010. National Governors Association Center for Best Practices and Council of Chief State School Officers. All rights reserved.
© Copyright 2007–2018. Texas Education Association (TEA). All rights reserved.

Shell Education

A division of Teacher Created Materials
5301 Oceanus Drive
Huntington Beach, CA 92649-1030
www.tcmpub.com/shell-education
ISBN 978-1-4258-1733-6
©2018 Shell Educational Publishing, Inc.

Table of Contents

Author's Note

I began to conceptualize the idea for interactive notetaking during a time in my career when I was seeking to change my classroom from a teacher-led classroom to a student-centered one. I knew that it was time for me to stop doing all the talking and thinking in my classroom. I decided that I wanted my students to create products that included not only the content they were learning but also their thoughts and reflections about this information. It was at this time that I began to try interactive notetaking strategies in my instruction. By using interactive notes, my students were challenged not only to absorb the information I was teaching but also to respond to it, reflect on it, make connections to other learning, summarize, synthesize, evaluate, and more. New learning was being recorded as lesson input, but the format of the interactive notetaking challenged me as a teacher to create meaningful opportunities and activities for students to respond to the learning in the form of student output. As students took more active roles in the learning process, I found that they were the ones leading the classroom. Not only that, but students were able to keep all the lesson information I gave them in class in one organized booklet. And they could respond to the new knowledge they acquired in that same booklet. I called this the *interactive notebook*.

The interactive notebook also provided me with many ways to differentiate my instruction to effectively meet the needs of the many different learning styles my students possessed. After years of experience, I realized that the children in my classroom learned in varied ways. Some students learned best by watching others, others learned best by reading or discussing ideas, and most of them learned by doing. No matter what learning styles my students preferred, by implementing interactive notetaking, I was able to meet the needs of everyone. The sense of pride students felt when their interactive notebooks began to grow and grow was beyond my highest expectations.

What Is an Interactive Notebook?

An interactive notebook can be created using any type of blank bound notebook (e.g., spiral notebook or a journal-style notebook). The pages of the notebook are then utilized to record new learning as well as students' responses to the learning. Many different strategies that are effective with the interactive notebook are provided in this resource. All the strategies in this resource can be used without implementing them in an interactive notebook. However, the best thing about the interactive notebook is that the lesson strategies and techniques are either created directly in the notebook itself, or students work to complete separate activity sheets and then glue those pages into the notebooks to create portfolios that help minimize the supplies needed for each lesson. Most lessons modeled in this resource require only basic materials, such as photocopied activity sheets, pens, pencils, paper, glue, scissors, paper plates, colored pencils, or markers.

When thinking about what an interactive notebook is, the key word to remember is the base word *active*. Keeping the concept of active learning in mind at all times will assist you when implementing these strategies in your classroom. The interactive notebook is not a place for students to simply copy notes or definitions. Instead, it is a place for students to respond to what they are learning. Interactive notebooks facilitate a notetaking process that allows students to record information in personal and meaningful ways.

Students will use their interactive notebooks to store information acquired in class for the purpose of referring to it and reflecting on it at a later time. Their notebooks become central locations for course content and information. As students create interactive notebooks, they also reflect on the information as it is presented in class. Interactive notebooks allow students to use teacher-supplied notes to analyze, compare and contrast, summarize, synthesize, apply, and more.

Additionally, the interactive notebook becomes a pathway for interactive discussion between students and teachers. In the interactive notebook format, students either write notes or do a guided activity. By asking students to reflect on the content taught using specific strategies, the teacher is able to informally check students' work to guide further instruction. This provides the teacher with data to plan student/teacher discussions about students' understanding of the content. Students no longer think of their notes as assignments for teachers to grade but as a tool they can use to review, study, and refer during class discussions. The interactive notebook also gives students opportunities to personalize their work and make sense of what they have learned. Since students have notes and reflections they can reference, they will feel more comfortable when asked to discuss their work with peers or with the teacher.

Using Interactive Notebooks for Content-Area Literacy

Interactive notetaking supports reading strategies across the content areas. As students add information into their notebooks, they have the opportunity to review, reflect, and respond to new information through reading, writing, listening, and speaking. Students practice reading strategies and writing skills as they make connections with texts. Students also develop listening and speaking skills as they participate in whole-class, small-group, and partner discussions related to text passages.

Literacy skills are critical to the academic success of every student, as they are central to content-area curriculum from early elementary years into the secondary grades. At-risk students, students with learning disabilities, and English language learners are more likely to demonstrate difficulties in literacy, particularly in comprehension and vocabulary acquisition (Barnatt n.d.).

One way to help bridge this gap is through informational texts. The term *informational text* refers to nonfiction text or non-narrative texts. The use of informational text supports content knowledge, opening doors to a variety of methods for students to learn about content-area topics. Informational text also allows students to explore a wide range of topics, make connections to prior experiences, and build new understandings of the world. Further, informational text is increasingly available across a range of reading abilities.

Many of the strategies in this resource use informational text to accomplish goals in literacy development. The goal of introducing these strategies is that teachers will discover many methods that can apply to any piece of informational text. Interactive notetaking creates opportunities to understand the structure and function of informational text. These activities also support the development of new vocabulary. By putting these interactive notes into notebooks, students create records of their learning and development.

Informational text should be a central part of literacy education to engage students, to provide explicit instruction across reading genres, and to build content knowledge. The need for students to build skills in understanding informational text is further underscored by today's college and career readiness standards. "Most of the required reading in college and workforce training programs is informational in structure and challenging in content; postsecondary education programs typically provide students with both a higher volume of such reading than is generally required in K–12 schools and comparatively little scaffolding" (National Governors Association Center for Best Practices and Council of Chief State School Officers 2010). To help students transition more effectively to the reading demands of college and careers, the standards call for increasing amounts of informational text integrated into English language arts classrooms as well as an increase in explicit literacy development in the content areas. The strategies in this resource support these needs.

Implementing Interactive Notebooks

Where and When to Use Interactive Notebooks

Interactive notebooks can be used anywhere, anytime, and in any content area! There is no right or wrong time or place to implement interactive notebooks. Primary grades can create "big" notebooks with poster board as a whole-class activity. These notebooks can be only a few pages that have a specific focus on one theme or unit and later placed in a reading center. Upper-elementary and secondary grades may choose to create content-specific interactive notebooks. A new notebook can be started at each grading period and then used to review for end-of-term exams. Elementary teachers may choose to create one notebook to be used across the content areas and organized by a daily log. With this type of interactive notebook, students start a new page every day, and all activities for that day are sequentially added to the notebook.

Interactive notebooks can also be used solely for vocabulary- or unit-based notebooks. A vocabulary notebook can best be thought of as a personal dictionary. This can be an effective tool for students to organize and manage their vocabulary learning by recording the words they encounter, their meanings, and any other aspects of the words deemed important for a particular content area or across disciplines. Unit-based interactive notebooks focus on one unit of study only. This type of interactive notebook is effective because it allows students to easily organize and archive their learning for a particular topic.

Components of Interactive Notebooks

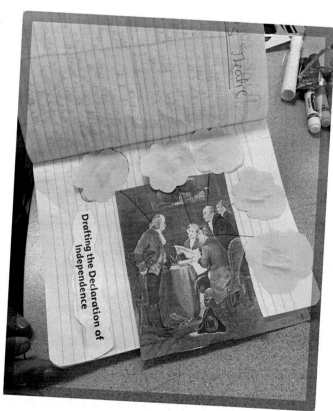

Have students set up interactive notebooks specific to your chosen requirements. The setup will depend on the grade level and the content to be included. There is no right or wrong way to do it. The goal simply is to be consistent throughout the notebook.

Most lessons in this book utilize two pages of the interactive notebook: the Lesson Input page and the Student Output page. You may set up these two pages in a left/right orientation (pages face each other) or a right/left orientation (one page is on the back of the other). However, it is important to keep the orientation consistent as much as possible.

Implementing Interactive Notebooks (cont.)

Components of Interactive Notebooks (cont.)

Lesson Input Page	Student Output Page
Student records new learning from the lesson.	Student reflects, reviews, revises, summarizes, and responds.
• class notes • discussion notes • handouts with new information • reading notes • graphic organizers • folded-paper notetaking guides	• process new ideas and connect to prior knowledge • reorganize new information in creative formats • express opinions and feelings • explore new ideas • summarize, synthesize • respond to new learning
One page of each lesson in the notebook is for input from the lesson itself. This includes class notes, discussion notes, and reading notes. Most of the information on this side is the "testable" information. The Lesson Input page can be a place for the teacher to model illustrated outlines, flow charts, annotated slides, T-charts, and other graphic organizers. Handouts and folded-paper notetaking guides with new information also go on the Lesson Input page.	One page of each lesson in the notebook is for student output. The student responds to new learning by using different strategies suggested by the teacher. The purpose of this page is for students to record what they have learned in their own words. Here, students can tap into their feelings and reactions to activities. By doing this, students can see how the new information fits into the bigger picture of the context and their prior knowledge.
The Lesson Input page allows teachers to: • follow gradual release to move students to the independent phase when introducing new learning. • organize information for students to process sequentially. • meet the needs of diverse learners by including graphic organizers, photos, time lines, written notes, and other forms to organize information.	The Student Output page allows students to: • connect new information to prior learning. • summarize, synthesize, analyze, and evaluate information they have learned. • respond to information by making personal connections.

Implementing Interactive Notebooks (cont.)

How to Set Up Interactive Notebooks

As a teacher, you have a lot of flexibility on how you choose to organize and utilize interactive notebooks within your classroom. Here are some elements to include in every interactive notebook regardless of the structure or purpose. These elements will help keep students' notebooks organized, assist students in meeting expectations, and provide the tools to help you assess student work.

➠ **Cover**—Encourage students to design covers for their interactive notebooks to reflect the content area(s) specific to the notebook. A title should also be included.

➠ **Student Guidelines**—Expectations of what is required in student notebooks (e.g., quality expectations, content expectations, effort expectations) should be clearly stated. Guidelines can be specific or flexible depending on your preference. These can be typed and then glued into the notebook or handwritten by students. Refer to the guidelines as often as needed to reinforce expectations.

➠ **Author Page**—Have each student create an author page. The author page could include a photograph and personal information, such as age, height, favorite foods, and family members. The author pages help students distinguish their notebooks from those of their classmates.

➠ **Table of Contents**—Have each student create a running table of contents for his or her notebook. Several pages should be designated for the table of contents. Students will add entries to the table of contents as they complete activities. This will allow you to locate activities more easily to grade or review the lessons. The table of contents can also be used to record grades by placing scores in the left-hand margin next to the activities.

➠ **Tabs**—One idea for organizing the various sections of a notebook is to use sticky notes as tabs. A sticky note can be placed in the top-right corner of the first page of each new section. The label for the section can be written at the edge of the sticky note. For example, a mathematics notebook might be set up with the following tabs: Table of Contents, Number Sense, Measurement, Geometry, Algebra, and Problem Solving. If the notebook will be used in all content areas, it could be set up with content-area tabs.

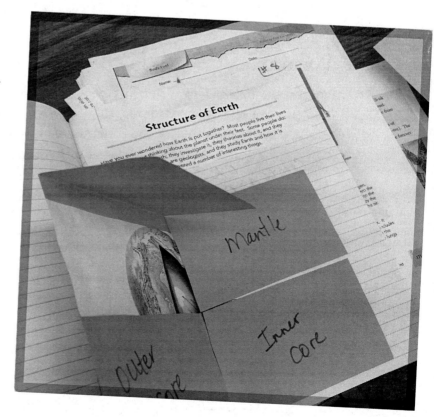

Strategies Overview

Interactive Notetaking for Content-Area Literacy provides teachers with notetaking strategies to support and extend student learning. Using interactive notebooks helps students organize their work in one place. This notebook becomes a bridge of communication between the student and the teacher, which provides a better atmosphere for a classroom environment. Interactive notebooks also help students become independent, creative thinkers and writers. This resource explains how to use a variety of strategies across the content areas. Each strategy is briefly explained on the next few pages.

Talking Partners

Talking Partners strategies allow students to engage in discussions in small groups or with partners about what they have learned. These strategies provide opportunities for students to develop their oral-language skills while focusing on academic language. They support the literacy components of speaking and listening. As the teacher, you can listen to student conversations and make informal assessments about their comprehension. Talking Partners strategies in this book include:

- Clock Partners
- Peer Partner Review
- Think-Pair-Square-Share

Vocabulary

Vocabulary strategies allow students to expand their content-area and academic vocabulary knowledge by illustrating word meanings, categorizing words, discussing vocabulary, and more. Students will have opportunities to write and review vocabulary that is introduced in the context of literature or content-area material. The goal is for students to use the content-area and academic vocabulary in their reading, writing, listening, and speaking. Vocabulary strategies in this book include:

- Chart and Match
- Four-Flap Vocabulary Book
- Frayer Model
- Pocket It!
- Word Web

Strategies Overview *(cont.)*

Activating Prior Knowledge

Activating Prior Knowledge strategies help students relate what they are learning to something they already know. When students are introduced to a new topic, they may need help making those connections. The goal of these strategies is to guide students to think about what is important about the new topic or concept and build background knowledge that will help them understand the content. Activating Prior Knowledge strategies in this book include:

- Find Your Corner
- KWL
- Possible Sentences
- Preview Log
- Skim and Post It

Summarizing

Summarizing strategies help students develop a system to organize class notes and material. Doing so provides a way to record the most important or relevant information from a lesson. These strategies help students recall more information from class discussions, lectures, and readings by developing active listening and purposeful notetaking skills. The goal is for students to realize the importance of notetaking as well as critical and careful listening. Summarizing strategies in this book include:

- Concept Map
- Four-Triangle Notetaking
- Inner/Outer Notes
- Three-Sides Notetaking
- Main Idea and Details

Strategies Overview (cont.)

Building Comprehension

Building Comprehension strategies help students develop their skills for active reading before, during, and after engaging with text. Students learn to chunk text, focus their attention on the most important ideas, summarize, compare and contrast, and make connections with the text. Building Comprehension strategies in this book include:

- Compare and Contrast
- Stop and Think
- Summary Wheel
- Three-Flap Notetaking

Review

Review strategies help students understand that it is important to not only take notes and participate in classroom learning but also to review regularly what they have learned in order to remember the information long term. Reviewing information in a variety of ways can help students accomplish this. Review strategies in this book include:

- Fact or Fib
- Reading-Review Web

Primary Sources

Primary Sources strategies give students tools to comprehend historical documents and images. Students will analyze primary sources in a variety of ways that will guide them toward higher-order thinking and improved analytical skills. The goal is for students to use their prior knowledge to engage with primary sources. Primary Sources strategies in this book include:

- Analyzing a Photograph

How to Use This Book

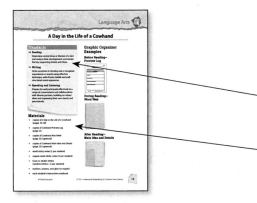

Lesson Structure

Each lesson includes the following components to establish the structure and flow:

- **Standards**—Each lesson is correlated to content-area standards.

- **Materials**—Materials are listed for each lesson. Most materials can be found easily in a classroom or school.

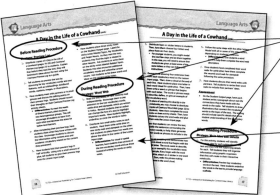

- **Procedure**—This section provides step-by-step instructions for teachers. Lessons include before-, during-, and after-reading activities. This structure supports student comprehension.

- **Differentiation**—Differentiation strategies are provided to help teachers meet the needs of diverse learners.

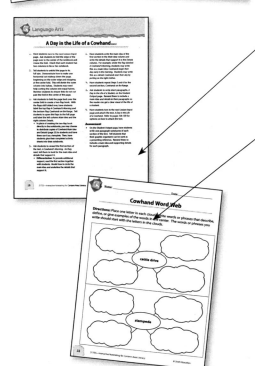

- **Assessment**—Assessment strategies are given for each activity in every lesson to measure student achievement. These strategies connect the content of the activities to Student Output tasks.

- **Student Reproducibles**—Each lesson includes reproducibles of the activity sheets or graphic organizers.

Digital Resources

The Digital Resources include blank templates of graphic organizers found throughout the book and standards correlations. A list of the Digital Resources can be found on page 160.

Introduction

Correlations to Standards

Shell Education is committed to producing educational materials that are research and standards based. In this effort, we have correlated all of our products to the academic standards of all 50 states, the District of Columbia, the Department of Defense Dependents Schools, and all Canadian provinces.

How to Find Standards Correlations

To print a customized correlation report of this product for your state, visit our website at **www.teachercreatedmaterials.com/administrators/correlations/** and follow the online directions. If you require assistance in printing correlation reports, please contact our Customer Service Department at 1-877-777-3450.

Purpose and Intent of Standards

The Every Student Succeeds Act (ESSA) mandates that all states adopt challenging academic standards that help students meet the goal of college and career readiness. While many states already adopted academic standards prior to ESSA, the act continues to hold states accountable for detailed and comprehensive standards. Standards are designed to focus instruction and guide adoption of curricula. Standards are statements that describe the criteria necessary for students to meet specific academic goals. They define the knowledge, skills, and content students should acquire at each level. Standards are also used to develop standardized tests to evaluate students' academic progress. Teachers are required to demonstrate how their lessons meet state standards. State standards are used in the development of our products, so educators can be assured they meet the academic requirements of each state.

College and Career Readiness

Today's College and Career Readiness (CCR) standards offer guidelines for preparing K–12 students with the knowledge and skills that are necessary to succeed in postsecondary job training and education. CCR standards include the Common Core State Standards (CCSS) as well as other state-adopted standards, such as the Texas Essential Knowledge and Skills (TEKS) and the Virginia Standards of Learning (SOL). The CCR standards listed in the Digital Resources support the objectives presented throughout the lessons.

McREL Compendium

Each year, McREL analyzes state standards and revises the compendium to produce a general compilation of national standards. The standards listed in the Digital Resources support the objectives presented throughout the lessons.

A Day in the Life of a Cowhand

Standards

⇢ **Reading**

Determine central ideas or themes of a text and analyze their development; summarize the key supporting details and ideas.

⇢ **Writing**

Write narratives to develop real or imagined experiences or events using effective technique, well-chosen details and well-structured event sequences.

⇢ **Speaking and Listening**

Prepare for and participate effectively in a range of conversations and collaborations with diverse partners, building on others' ideas and expressing their own clearly and persuasively.

Materials

- copies of *A Day in the Life of a Cowhand* (pages 19–20)

- copies of *Cowhand Preview Log* (page 21)

- copies of *Cowhand Word Web* (page 22) (optional)

- copies of *Cowhand Main Idea and Details* (page 23) (optional)

- small sticky notes (2 per student)

- regular-sized sticky notes (3 per student)

- foam or sticker letters (random letters—4 per student)

- markers, scissors, and glue (or stapler)

- each student's interactive notebook

Graphic Organizer Examples

Before Reading— Preview Log

During Reading— Word Web

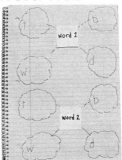

After Reading— Main Idea and Details

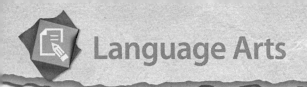

A Day in the Life of a Cowhand (cont.)

Before Reading Procedure

Strategy: Preview Log

1. Distribute copies of *A Day in the Life of a Cowhand* (pages 19–20) and *Cowhand Preview Log* (page 21) to students. Explain that before they read the text, they will brainstorm ideas about the text using the *Cowhand Preview Log* as a guide.

2. Tell students to preview the text by skimming for key vocabulary words and text features, such as subheadings, boldfaced words, captions, images, or illustrations.

3. Have students meet with partners or in small groups and discuss the talking points on their preview logs. Students should record their thoughts on their *Cowhand Preview Log* activity sheets.
   - **Differentiation:** To meet the needs of diverse learners, place students into heterogeneous groups. This will encourage all students to learn from each other and decrease the stress for below-level learners.

4. After completing their preview logs, have students share what they have written with the class. Encourage students to discuss the information using content-area and academic vocabulary related to the content they previewed.

5. Have students fold their preview logs in half vertically. Using only a small amount of glue, tell students to glue their preview logs onto the Lesson Input page.

Assessment

- Have students place three sticky notes on the Student Output page. Label the sticky notes *Related Topics*, *Key Vocabulary*, and *Proper Nouns*. As they read the text, students may find the topic is related to other lessons. Ask students to write these on the sticky notes labeled *Related Topics*. Students may also encounter additional vocabulary words and unfamiliar proper nouns. Ask students to list these words and ideas on the correct sticky notes.

During Reading Procedure

Strategy: Word Web

1. Read the text aloud, or have students read independently. Encourage them to pay attention to the two vocabulary words, *cattle drive* and *stampede*, which are written in italics. Remind students that an author can change the font of a text to highlight important words. Have students highlight, underline, or circle the words in italics.

2. Distribute two small sticky notes to each student. Have them write *cattle drive* on one sticky note and *stampede* on the other. Ask students to place those two words one above the other in the center of the Lesson Input page.
   - **Differentiation:** For visual or spatial learners, have students draw pictures of the two vocabulary words and use those instead of writing the words on sticky notes.

A Day in the Life of a Cowhand (cont.)

crayons - write random letters

3. Distribute foam or sticker letters to students. Then, have them choose four letters and place them on their desks.
   - For younger students, you might model the next few steps and do them together. In this case, you will need to ensure that students are given at least some of the same letters so they can follow your instructions.

4. Demonstrate drawing four extension lines from each vocabulary word on the Lesson Input page. Then, draw a cloud at the end of each line. Have students place one letter in each word cloud for *cattle drive*. Then, have them write a word or phrase that begins with each letter. The word or phrase needs to describe, define, or give an example of the vocabulary word.
   - In place of creating this directly in the notebooks, you may choose to distribute copies of *Cowhand Word Web* (page 22) to students. Have them complete the word webs on their activity sheets. Then, have students cut out the word webs and glue them onto the Lesson Input page.

5. Explain that students can review the text, especially the sentences surrounding the vocabulary words, to help them generate ideas for words or phrases to include in the clouds.
   - If you are modeling this, demonstrate how to think about a word that begins with the target letter. The word needs to describe, define, or exemplify the vocabulary word. For example, if you begin with the word *cattle drive*, attach an *m* sticker in one word cloud. Then, write the phrase *making cattle move* in the word cloud.

6. Follow the same steps with the other letters. Model with all or some of the other letters, depending on students' readiness.
   - **Differentiation:** Give students a word bank to help them complete the word web descriptors.

7. Once students have completed their word webs for *cattle drive*, have them complete the second word web for *stampede* following the same procedure.

8. Have students discuss their word webs with partners. Tell students to revise their word webs to include their partners' ideas.

Assessment

- On the Student Output page, have each student write a paragraph about real-life connections they have made with the words in the webs. Tell students to draw illustrations that connect the vocabulary words to the topic of the text. The writing should include specific details that show student understanding of the vocabulary words.

After Reading Procedure

Strategy: Main Idea and Details

1. For this activity, students will identify the main idea for each subheading in the text and then find the supporting details for each. Tell students they will organize information using graphic organizers that they will create in their interactive notebooks.
   - **Differentiation:** Preview key vocabulary words in the text. Have students underline key words in the text to provide language scaffolds.

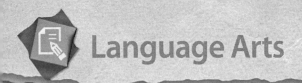

A Day in the Life of a Cowhand *(cont.)*

2. Have students turn to the next Lesson Input page. Ask students to fold the edge of the page over to the center of the notebook and crease the fold. Check that each student has two columns in his or her notebook.

3. Tell students to unfold the page to its full size. Demonstrate how to make one horizontal cut midway down the page, beginning on the outer edge and stopping at the center fold. This will divide the outer column into halves. Students may need help cutting the column into equal halves. Monitor students to ensure they do not cut past the fold in the center of the page.

4. Ask students to fold the page back over the center fold to create a two-flap book. With the flaps still folded over, have students label the top flap *A Cowhand's Morning* and the bottom flap *Cowhands on the Range*. Tell students to open the flaps to the full page and label the left column *Main Idea* and the right column *Details*.
   - In place of creating the two-flap book directly in the notebooks, you may choose to distribute copies of *Cowhand Main Idea and Details* (page 23) to students and have them use it as a template. Then, have students glue their completed activity sheets into their notebooks.

5. Ask students to reread the first section of the text, *A Cowhand's Morning*. As they read, tell them to look for the main idea and details that support it.
   - **Differentiation:** To provide additional support, read the first section together with students. Model how to circle the main idea and underline the details that support it.

6. Have students write the main idea of the first section in the *Main Idea* column and write the details that support it in the *Details* column. For example, under the flap labeled *A Cowhand's Morning*, students may write this as a main idea: *Cowhands begin their day early in the morning.* Students may write this as a detail: *Cowhands start their day by putting on the right clothes.*

7. Have students repeat Steps 5 and 6 for the second section, *Cowhands on the Range*.

8. Ask students to write short paragraphs, *A Day in the Life of a Student*, on the Student Output page. Remind them to include a main idea and details in their paragraphs so the reader can get a clear visual of the life of a student.

9. Have students turn to the next Lesson Input page and attach the text, *A Day in the Life of a Cowhand*. Refer to pages 158–159 for options on how to attach the text.

Assessment

- On the Student Output page, have students write one-paragraph summaries of each section of the text. Tell students that their graphic organizers can be used as a prewriting reference. Remind them to include a main idea and supporting details for each paragraph.

Excerpt from *Black Beauty*

Standards

➠ **Reading**

Determine central ideas or themes of a text and analyze their development; summarize the key supporting details and ideas.

➠ **Writing**

Produce clear and coherent writing in which the development, organization, and style are appropriate to task, purpose, and audience.

➠ **Speaking and Listening**

Prepare for and participate effectively in a range of conversations and collaborations with diverse partners, building on others' ideas and expressing their own clearly and persuasively.

Materials

- copies of *Excerpt from Black Beauty* (pages 29–30)

- copies of *Black Beauty Find Your Corner* (page 31) (optional)

- copies of *Black Beauty Three-Flap Notetaking* (page 32) (optional)

- 4 large poster charts

- 10-inch sealed envelopes (1 per student)

- index cards (16 per student)

- 8.5" x 11" paper (1 per student)

- markers, scissors, and glue (or stapler)

- each student's interactive notebook

Graphic Organizer Examples

Before Reading— Find Your Corner

During Reading— Pocket It!

After Reading— Three-Flap Notetaking

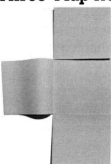

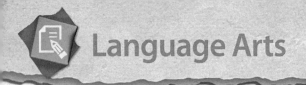

Excerpt from *Black Beauty* (cont.)

Before Reading Procedure

Strategy: Find Your Corner

1. Before beginning the lesson, write each of the following sentence stems on one of the posters: *I am brand new…; I know a little…; I know more than a little, but I am not an expert…*; and *I am an expert….* Hang one poster in each of the four corners of the room.

2. Have students turn to the next Lesson Input page. Ask each student to draw a vertical line down the center of the page and a horizontal line across the center of the page.
   - In place of creating this directly in the notebooks, you may choose to distribute copies of *Black Beauty Find Your Corner* (page 31) to students. Have them cut out the table at the end of the activity and glue it onto the Lesson Input page.

3. Draw students' attention to the four posters. Ask them to label each square on their page to match each poster.

4. Introduce the topic of the Black Beauty series of books. Depending on students' levels of knowledge, you could have a brief discussion about some famous fiction and nonfiction horses, such as Black Beauty or Flicka. You may also choose to display some pictures or preview the text with students. Provide students time to think about the topic of horses, such as Black Beauty.

5. Ask each student to decide which poster applies to his or her level of prior knowledge. Then, have them each justify why they chose their level by writing notes in the correct corner of the page.
   - **Differentiation:** Provide students with sentence stems to help them describe their prior knowledge. Provide a word bank to help students complete the sentences.

6. Tell students to move to the corner of the room with the poster that matches their levels of prior knowledge. Students should bring their notebooks with them. Then, have students discuss with their poster groups why they each chose that poster.

7. After the group discussion, have students return to their desks. Tell students that they will refer back to this graphic organizer at the end of the lesson.

Assessment

- On the Student Output page, have students write any new information or questions they might have after talking with their fellow classmates.

During Reading Procedure

Strategy: Pocket It!

1. Write the following words on the board: *colt, halter, headstall, bit, bridle, coaxing, girth*, and *blacksmith*. Read the words aloud. Have students repeat the words. Explain that they will read about and complete an activity with these words.

Excerpt from *Black Beauty* (cont.)

2. Read aloud *Excerpt from Black Beauty* (pages 29–30) to students, or read it together as a choral read. Point out the vocabulary words as you read. Tell students to underline or highlight the words.

3. Distribute one sealed envelope to each student. Have students hold the envelopes vertically, fold them in half using a horizontal fold, and crease the fold.

4. Model how to cut the envelope into two halves by cutting along the creased fold. By cutting the fold, they should create two pockets. Have students keep one pocket for the activity, and collect the second pocket for future activities.

5. Have students label their pockets *Black Beauty Vocabulary*, and glue them onto their Lesson Input pages.

6. Distribute 16 index cards to each student. Tell students to write the words from the board on one side of eight of the index cards. Then, have them draw illustrations of each vocabulary word on the opposite side. For example: On the front of one index card, write the word *colt*. On the back, draw or sketch a young horse. You may need to model the first word card.

7. Ask students to next write the definition of each word on an index card. They should place all their cards in their interactive notebook pockets.

8. Explain that they will reread the text independently or with partners and will focus on the remaining vocabulary words.

9. Have students mix up the cards to use as review. Each student can then work in a group or with a partner to quiz one another. They should select index cards, read the words on the cards, look at the illustrations, and discuss which definition cards match the words. Students could also play a matching game by laying all the cards facedown and matching each word/illustration to the correct definition.

   - **Differentiation:** Divide the class into several small, heterogeneous groups. Provide illustrations for each of the vocabulary words. Encourage students to work in groups to identify which picture matches each vocabulary word. Have students glue the illustrations on the fronts of the index cards next to the vocabulary words.

Assessment

- Assess students by making observations as they quiz each other in partners or in groups.

- Have students write short paragraphs on their Student Output pages describing the concept of "breaking in" a horse. Review students' writing to determine whether vocabulary words are used properly.

After Reading Procedure

Strategy: Three-Flap Notetaking

1. Tell students to reread the text. Explain that they should focus on creating strong mental pictures of the steps that Black Beauty took during her "breaking in" phase. This is called *visualizing*.

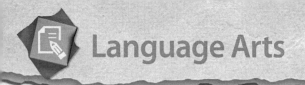

Excerpt from *Black Beauty* (cont.)

2. Have students highlight or underline the three main steps it takes to "break in" a horse. Consider modeling how to decide upon the steps by thinking aloud about what the most important ideas are for each step.

3. Distribute sheets of 8.5" x 11" paper to students. Ask students to hold the paper portrait style and make one vertical fold. Then, fold it again into thirds with two horizontal folds. Tell students to open the horizontal folds to show three sections. Then, have them open the vertical fold and make two cuts along the horizontal folds, stopping at the vertical fold. This should create three flaps. Monitor students to ensure that they do not cut past the fold in the center of the page. Have students label the flaps from top to bottom, *Step 1*, *Step 2*, and *Step 3*.
   - In place of creating this graphic organizer from scratch, you may choose to distribute copies of *Black Beauty Three-Flap Notetaking* (page 32) to students. Have them follow the same instructions as in Step 3.

4. Tell students to think about the main idea of each step in the process of "breaking in" a horse. Explain that students will label the three outside flaps with the three steps to "break in" a horse. For example, next to *Step 1*, they might write *Place the bit and bridle*. Next to *Step 2*, *Wear a saddle*, and then *Step 3*, *Put on iron shoes*.

5. Have students write the details about each step behind the correct flap.
   - **Differentiation:** Place students into heterogeneous groups. Encourage students to work together and discuss what they are going to write as explanations for each step. Provide sentence stems or word banks as extra support.

6. Ask students to share their ideas about each step of the "breaking in" process with partners. Encourage them to revise their own work based on the discussion to make it more detailed. Tell students to turn to the next Lesson Input page and glue their folded graphic organizers. If needed, students can crease along the horizontal folds and glue only the center section of their graphic organizers into the notebook. This will allow the page to fit better into their notebooks. Then, students can fold the top and bottom flaps in towards the center.

7. Have students turn to the next Lesson Input page and attach the text, *Excerpt from Black Beauty*. Refer to pages 158–159 for options on how to attach the text.

Assessment

- Have students revisit the Student Output page of the Find Your Corner activity. Ask students to write a few sentences about what they learned about horses in general and specifically what they learned about Black Beauty. Have students discuss how the things they learned helped them understand how and what horses must do during the "breaking in" phase. Students should include specific details or events from the text that contributed to the "breaking in" of Black Beauty.

Excerpt from *Black Beauty*

By Anna Sewell

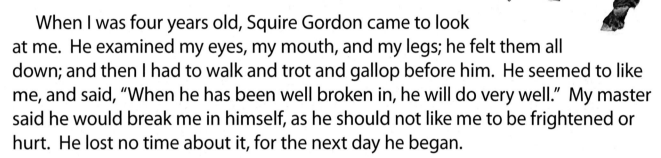

I was now beginning to grow handsome; my coat had grown fine and soft, and was bright black. I had one white foot and a pretty white star on my forehead. I was thought very handsome, but my master would not sell me until I was four years old because he said lads ought not to work like men, and colts ought not to work like horses until they were quite grown up.

When I was four years old, Squire Gordon came to look at me. He examined my eyes, my mouth, and my legs; he felt them all down; and then I had to walk and trot and gallop before him. He seemed to like me, and said, "When he has been well broken in, he will do very well." My master said he would break me in himself, as he should not like me to be frightened or hurt. He lost no time about it, for the next day he began.

Because not everyone may know what breaking in is, I will describe it. It means to teach a horse to wear a saddle and bridle, and to carry on his back a man, woman, or child; to go just the way they wish, and to go quietly. So you understand, this breaking in is a thing of great importance.

I had, of course, long been used to a halter and a headstall, and to be led about in the fields and lanes quietly, but now I was to have a bit and bridle. My master gave me some oats as usual, and after a good deal of coaxing, he got the bit into my mouth and the bridle fixed, but it was a nasty thing! Those who have never had a bit in their mouths cannot think how terrible it feels—a great piece of cold, hard steel as thick as a man's finger to be pushed into one's mouth, between one's teeth, and over one's tongue. The ends come out at the corner of your mouth and are held fast there by straps over your head, under your throat, round your nose, and under your chin. There is no way in the world you can get rid of the nasty hard thing; it is very bad—yes, very bad—at least I thought so. But I knew my mother always wore one when she went out, and all horses did when they were grown up. And so, with the nice oats and with my master's pats, kind words, and gentle ways, I got to wear my bit and bridle.

Excerpt from *Black Beauty* (cont.)

Next came the saddle, but that was not half so bad; my master placed it on my back very gently, while old Daniel held my head. He then made the girths fast under my body, patting and talking to me all the time; then I had a few oats, then a little leading about. This he did every day until I began to look for the oats and the saddle. At length, one morning, my master got on my back and rode me round the meadow on the soft grass. It certainly did feel strange, but I must say I felt rather proud to carry my master, and as he continued to ride me a little every day, I soon became accustomed to it.

The next unpleasant business was putting on the iron shoes; that too was quite difficult at first. My master went with me to the blacksmith's forge, to see that I was not hurt or frightened. The blacksmith took my feet in his hand, one after the other, and cut away some of the hoof. It did not pain me, so I stood still on three legs until he had done them all. Then he took a piece of iron the shape of my foot, clapped it on, and drove some nails through the shoe quite into my hoof, so that the shoe was firmly on. My feet felt very stiff and heavy, but in time I got used to it.

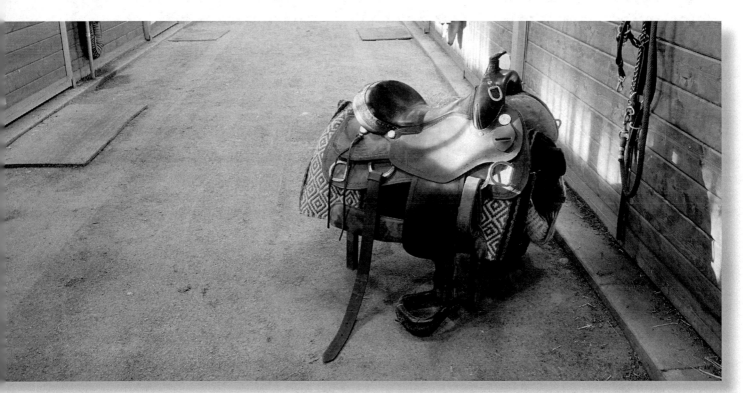

Black Beauty Find Your Corner

Directions: Decide which corner best describes your prior knowledge of horses. In that corner, write a few sentences explaining why you chose it.

Horses	
I am brand new…	I am an expert…
I know a little…	I know more than a little, but I am not an expert…

Name: _____ Date:_____

Black Beauty Three-Flap Notetaking

Directions: Cut out the graphic organizer. Fold it in half along the vertical line. Then, cut along the two horizontal lines. Be sure not to cut past the fold. Fold the flaps over.

History's Mysteries

Standards

➤ Reading

Determine central ideas or themes of a text and analyze their development; summarize the key supporting details and ideas.

➤ Writing

Produce clear and coherent writing in which the development, organization, and style are appropriate to task, purpose, and audience.

➤ Speaking and Listening

Prepare for and participate effectively in a range of conversations and collaborations with diverse partners, building on others' ideas and expressing their own clearly and persuasively.

Materials

- copies of *History's Mysteries* (pages 37–38)

- copies of *History's Mysteries Think-Pair-Square-Share* (page 39)

- copies of *History's Mysteries Compare and Contrast* (page 40) (optional)

- copies of *History's Mysteries Inner/Outer Notes* (page 41) (optional)

- poster chart (1 per group; optional)

- small sticky notes (1 per student)

- uncoated paper plates (1 per student)

- markers, scissors, and glue (or stapler)

- each student's interactive notebook

Graphic Organizer Examples

Before Reading—Think-Pair-Square-Share

During Reading—Compare and Contrast

After Reading—Inner/Outer Notes

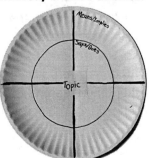

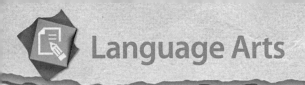

History's Mysteries (cont.)

Before Reading Procedure

Strategy: Think-Pair-Square-Share

1. Distribute copies of *History's Mysteries Think-Pair-Square-Share* (page 39) to students. Write the following questions on the board: *What are the job descriptions of being a historian and a detective? How are historians and detectives alike?*

2. Ask students to think about the questions. Have students record their answers in the *Think* box on the activity sheet.

3. Tell students to share their answers with the person next to them. Pairs of students should collaborate to find the best answer to share with other classmates and an explanation of why each is the best. Then, have each pair write their answer and explanation in the *Pair* box on the activity sheet.

4. Have students share their answers in groups of four or more. Have each pair share their answers with the group. Then, each group should decide which answer they think is best as well as an explanation of their reasoning. Once an answer has been agreed upon, students should write their group's answer and the justification in the *Square* box on the activity sheet.
   - **Differentiation:** Once the Square groups have agreed upon their best answers to share with the class, ask students to transfer their group answers to a poster chart. Each group could then present its answer to the rest of the class. You may choose for the class to do a gallery walk so they can get a closer look at each group's presentation.

5. Ask students to share their group choices and reasoning with the class. Have students write the best answers they heard along with explanations defending their choices in the *Share* box on the activity sheet.

6. Have students fold their activity sheets into quarters. Tell them to glue the bottom-right quarter of the completed *History's Mysteries Think-Pair-Square-Share* activity sheet onto an empty Lesson Input page.

7. On the Student Output page, have students write summaries of their discussions. Tell students to include their final answers and why they chose them.

Assessment

- On the Student Output page, have students compose paragraphs that express their final answers. Have students use the notes they took from the various groups to compile cohesive paragraphs. Remind students that they should explain their final answers in detail.

During Reading Procedure

Strategy: Compare and Contrast

1. Distribute copies of *History's Mysteries* (pages 37–38) to students. Read the text aloud, or have students read with partners. After students have finished reading, explain that they will create graphic organizers in their interactive notebooks. They will use them to organize information to compare and contrast historians and detectives.

History's Mysteries (cont.)

2. Tell students to turn to the next Lesson Input page. Have students fold the edge of the page over to the center of the notebook and crease the fold. Check that all students have two columns in their notebooks.

3. Have students unfold the pages to their full size. Students should then make two cuts beginning on the outer edge and stopping at the center fold. This will divide the outer column into thirds. Monitor students to ensure that they do not cut past the fold in the center.
   - In place of creating this directly in the notebooks, you may choose to distribute copies of *History's Mysteries Compare and Contrast* (page 40) to students. Have them follow the same instructions as in Steps 2 and 3. Tell students to turn to the next Lesson Input page and glue their graphic organizers to it. If needed, students can fold down and glue only one section of their graphic organizers for a better fit.

4. Ask students to fold the page back over the center fold to create a three-flap book. With the flaps still folded over, have students label the top flap *Historians* and the bottom flap *Detectives*. Students should then label the middle flap *Compare*.

5. Tell students to think about what is unique to each of these professions. Tell them to write their ideas under the top and bottom flaps of their graphic organizers.
   - **Differentiation:** Scaffold this activity by varying the number of expected responses on students' graphic organizers. Or, alternatively, provide sentence stems.

6. Ask students to share their ideas about characteristics of historians. Make a list of students' ideas on the board. Repeat this procedure with the characteristics of detectives. Students should record these ideas in the corresponding sections of their graphic organizers.

7. Ask students to consider what historians and detectives have in common. Explain that this is what it means to compare two ideas. Tell students to list their ideas in the middle sections of their graphic organizers. Record student ideas on the board. Students should generate responses such as *both use primary sources to answer a series of questions* and *both have to prove that their answers are correct*. Have students record notes from the board in the *Compare* sections of their graphic organizers.

Assessment

- Have students review the information they listed under each flap. On the Student Output page, have students explain what is unique about historians and detectives. Then, have them explain what the two types of professions have in common.

After Reading Procedure

Strategy: Inner/Outer Notes

1. Distribute a paper plate and a small sticky note to each student. Ask students to fold the paper plate into four equal sections and trace all the folds.

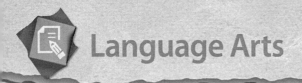

History's Mysteries (cont.)

2. Have each student place the sticky note in the center of the paper plate and write *History's Mysteries* on the sticky note. Then, ask each student to draw a circle just inside the rough edge of the paper plate. This will create an inner circle and an outer circle. Finally, have students label the inner circle *Says/Does* and the outer circle *Means/Implies*. Explain the meaning of the word *implies*, if necessary.

   - In place of creating this on paper plates, you may choose to distribute copies of *History's Mysteries Inner/Outer Notes* (page 41) to students. Once finished, tell students to turn to the next Lesson Input page and glue their graphic organizers.

3. Tell students that they are going to read the *History's Mysteries* text one more time. Ask students to take notes on each section. Model how to record a few key ideas about Masked Prisoner in the first section's inner circle. For example, you might write, *The masked prisoner's name was Eustache Dauger*, in the inner circle.

4. Think aloud what this means or implies, and record this in the outer circle. You might explain that this means or implies, *Dauger was not allowed to show his face. No one knows who he was or why he was jailed.*

5. Continue reading as a class, or encourage students to finish reading independently. Each section of the students' plates should refer to one of the sections of the text. When students are finished, the plates should be fully completed.

   - **Differentiation:** Provide slips of paper with prewritten or pre-typed text that belongs in the inner and outer circles. Have students place each slip in the correct circle.

6. Pair students to share their information with partners. As students are talking about their inner/outer notes, encourage them to explain their reasoning.

7. Ask students to fold their paper plates in half and glue one half onto the next Lesson Input page.

8. On the Student Output page, have students use the information they learned from the text to explain which of the mysteries they would like to investigate. Challenge students to research the mystery and write any other details they learned.

9. Have students turn to the next Lesson Input page and attach the text, *History's Mysteries*. Refer to pages 158–159 for options on how to attach the text.

Assessment

- On the Student Output page, have students write short summary paragraphs about each of the mysteries from the text, including details from the information listed in their inner/outer notes.

History's Mysteries

Masked Prisoner

From around 1669 until his death in 1703, a mystery man was held in jails in France. Most of the time, he was in the Bastille. No one ever saw the man's face. It was always covered with a black velvet mask. The prisoner's name was Eustache Dauger. That is probably not his real name. Dauger was told he could not talk about himself. If he did, he would have been killed. Only the head of the Bastille was allowed to see his face. No one knows who he was or why he was jailed. Many people believe the prisoner was the brother of King Louis XIV. He may have even been a twin brother. They think Louis XIV jailed him. With Dauger in jail, no one could stop Louis from being the king.

Vanishing Act

The Bermuda Triangle is a place where dozens of boats, planes, and people have vanished. It is in the Atlantic Ocean. Some people think this area is very dangerous. They think there is a magnetic field there that causes compasses to stop working. Others think the strong water currents and bad weather are the reason for the danger.

In 1945, five U.S. Navy bombers flew out of Florida on a training flight. The pilots became lost within the Bermuda Triangle. Through one of the plane's radios, the leader of the group said his compass was off. He said everything looked strange. He couldn't figure out where they were. Another plane was sent out to find them, but it also vanished. The Navy called for all boats and planes in the area to look for them. But they were never found.

History's Mysteries (cont.)

Anastasia

There was big trouble in Russia in the early 1900s. The people wanted to get rid of the old rulers. Nicholas II was the ruler at the time. He was married and had five children. Anastasia was his youngest daughter. On July 17, 1918, the secret police killed Nicholas and his family. But did Anastasia survive? For years, many people thought so. Several women claimed that each was the lost duchess. They each stepped forward to claim the family fortune. But in 2009, science proved them all wrong. It is certain that the whole family died that day.

Bigfoot

Many people in the Pacific Northwest claim to have seen a giant, apelike, wild man. They say he roams through the forest. They claim he walks upright, is more than seven feet tall, and has huge feet. Some people have taken photos of an apelike man. But no one can tell for sure if it is a real creature or just a person in an ape suit! Some scientists think Bigfoot may be real.

Bigfoot is also called Sasquatch. This comes from a Salish Indian word meaning "wild man." Stories of wild men were told among the native people of the Pacific Northwest for centuries. J. W. Burns first wrote the stories down in the 1920s. He was the first to call the creature Sasquatch.

History's Mysteries Think-Pair-Square-Share

Directions: Complete the table with information from the text.

Think 	Pair 
Think of your answer. Write or draw your answer.	Talk with your partner. Write or draw your answer.
Square Meet with your group. Write or draw the best answer.	**Share** Listen to the groups. Decide on the best answer. Write or draw this answer.

History's Mysteries Compare and Contrast

Directions: Cut out the graphic organizer. Fold it in half along the vertical line. Then, cut along the two horizontal lines. Be sure not to cut past the fold. Fold the flaps over.

Name: _____ Date: _____

History's Mysteries Inner/Outer Notes

Directions: Record key ideas from the text in the inner circle. Write what each idea means or implies in the outer circle.

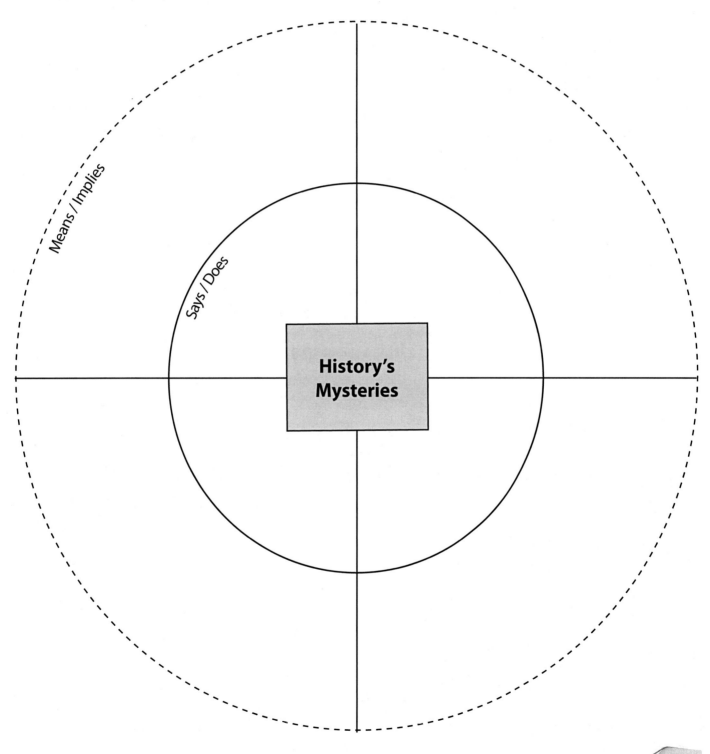

My Lemonade Stand

Standards

➤ Mathematics

Use place value understanding and properties of operations to perform multi-digit arithmetic.

➤ Reading

Interpret words and phrases as they are used in a text, including determining technical, connotative, and figurative meanings, and analyze how specific word choices shape meaning or tone.

➤ Writing

Produce clear and coherent writing in which the development, organization, and style are appropriate to task, purpose, and audience.

Materials

- copies of *My Lemonade Stand* (pages 47–48)

- copies of *My Lemonade Stand Word Web* (page 49) (optional)

- copies of *My Lemonade Stand Summary Wheel* (page 50) (optional)

- copies of *My Lemonade Stand Compare and Contrast* (page 51) (optional)

- small sticky notes (2 per student)

- foam or sticker letters (4 per student)

- uncoated paper plates (1 per student)

- markers, scissors, and glue (or stapler)

- each student's interactive notebook

Graphic Organizer Examples

Before Reading— Word Web

During Reading— Summary Wheel

After Reading— Compare and Contrast

My Lemonade Stand (cont.)

Before Reading Procedure

Strategy: Word Web

1. Distribute copies of *My Lemonade Stand* (pages 47–48) to students. Have them skim the text and find the two italicized words, *income* and *profit*. Remind students that an author can change the font of a text to highlight important words. Review the terms with students, and have them highlight, underline, or circle the words in italics.

2. Distribute two small sticky notes to each student. Have them write *income* on one sticky note and *profit* on the other. Have students place the words one above the other in the center of the Lesson Input page.
   - **Differentiation:** Have students draw pictures of the two vocabulary words and use those instead of writing the words on sticky notes.

3. Distribute four foam or sticker letters to each student.
   - For younger students, model the next few steps and do them together as a class. In this case, you will need to ensure that students are given at least some of the same letters so that students can follow your instructions.

4. Demonstrate drawing four extension lines from each vocabulary word on the Lesson Input page. Then, draw a cloud at the end of each line.

5. Have students place one letter in each word cloud for *income*. Then, have them write a word or phrase that begins with that letter. The word or phrase needs to describe, define, or give an example of the vocabulary word.
   - In place of creating this directly in the notebooks, you may choose to distribute copies of *My Lemonade Stand Word Web* (page 49) to students. Have them complete the word webs on their activity sheets. Then, have students cut out the word webs and glue them onto the Lesson Input page.

6. Explain that students can review the text, especially the sentences surrounding the vocabulary words, to help them generate ideas for words or phrases to include in the clouds.
   - If you are modeling this, demonstrate how to think about a word that begins with the target letter. The word needs to describe, define, or exemplify the vocabulary word. For example, if you begin with the word *income*, attach an *m* sticker in one word cloud. Then, write the phrase *making money* in the word cloud.

7. Follow the same steps with the other letters. Model with all or some of the other letters, depending on students' readiness.
   - **Differentiation:** For students who struggle with basic vocabulary, provide a word bank to help them complete the word web descriptors.

8. Once students have completed their word webs for *income*, have them complete the second word web for *profit* following the same procedure.

My Lemonade Stand (cont.)

9. Have students discuss their word webs with partners. Tell students to revise their word webs to include their partners' ideas.

Assessment

- On the Student Output page, have each student write a paragraph about real-life connections they have made with the words in the webs. Tell students to draw illustrations that connect the vocabulary words to the topic of the text. The writing should include specific details that show student understanding of the vocabulary words.

- If time allows, have students find pictures of real-life examples and glue them in their notebooks as part of their descriptions.

During Reading Procedure

Strategy: Summary Wheel

1. Distribute a paper plate to each student. Ask students to fold the paper plates into four sections. To do so, have students fold the paper plates in half and crease the folds. Then, fold the half into two equal sections by folding the top of the fold down to the bottom of the fold. The completed plates should look like pies with four slices.

2. Have students unfold their plates and trace the folds to create four sections. Explain that these are like spokes on a wheel.

3. Have students label the sections near the outer edge of the paper plates with the following words: *Day 1: My First Sale*, *Day 2: Ice*, *Day 3: Jill Murray*, *Day 4: My Secret Weapon*. Tell students that these are the most essential pieces of the text that will enable them to create summaries.

   - In place of using paper plates, you may choose to distribute copies of *My Lemonade Stand Summary Wheel* (page 50) to students. Have them complete the summary wheels on their activity sheets. Then, have students cut out the graphic organizers and glue them onto the Lesson Input side of their interactive notebooks.

4. Have students read the text as a guided reading activity. Pause during the reading to model how to add information to students' summary wheels. Details found in the text should be recorded in the corresponding wheel section.

   - Alternatively, you may choose to have students read independently and record information and details while they read.
   - **Differentiation:** Have students write entries in the summary wheel that are appropriate for their skill levels. This may mean that certain students draw pictures, write only a few words, write shorter examples, or work with partners to understand *income* and *profit*.

5. After students complete their wheels, have them fold the paper plates in half and glue them onto the next Lesson Input page so the folded sides are lined up to the red margin. Then, have students write the title, *My Lemonade Stand*, on the top of the folded paper plates.

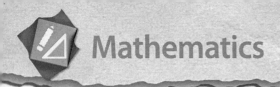

My Lemonade Stand (cont.)

Assessment

- Have students write summaries of the text on the Student Output page. Have them include the mathematical operations necessary to understand *income* and *profit*.

After Reading Procedure

Strategy: Compare and Contrast

1. Have students turn to the next Lesson Input page. Have them fold the edge of the page over to the center of the notebook and crease the fold. Check that all students have two columns in their notebooks.

2. Have students unfold the pages to their full size. Students should then make two cuts beginning on the outer edge and stopping at the center fold. This will divide the outer column into thirds. Monitor students so they do not cut past the fold in the center of the page.
   - In place of creating this directly in the notebooks, you may choose to distribute copies of *My Lemonade Stand Compare and Contrast* (page 51) to students. Have them follow the same instructions as in Steps 1 through 3. Tell students to turn to the next Lesson Input page and glue their graphic organizers. If needed, students can fold down and glue only one section of their graphic organizers for a better fit.

3. Ask students to fold the page back over to the center fold to create a three-flap book. With the flaps still folded over, have students label the top flap *Income* and the bottom flap *Profit*. Students should then label the middle flap *Compare*.

4. Tell students to think about what each of these concepts means or what characteristics are unique to each concept. Tell them to write their ideas under the top and bottom flaps of their graphic organizers.
   - **Differentiation:** Scaffold this activity by changing the number of expected responses on the graphic organizers. Or provide sentence stems if needed.

5. Ask students to share their ideas about characteristics of income. Make a list of students' ideas on the board. Some ideas may include: *revenue*, *pay*, and *salary*. Repeat this procedure with the characteristics of profit. Some ideas may include: *earnings*, *takings*, and *income*. Students should record these ideas in the corresponding sections of their graphic organizers.

6. Ask students to consider what income and profit have in common. Explain that this is what it means to compare two ideas. Have them list their ideas in the middle section of their graphic organizers. Record their ideas on the board. Students should generate responses, such as *both have to do with money*, and *both have to do with income*. Have students record these in the *Compare* section of their graphic organizers.

7. Have students turn to the next Lesson Input page and attach the text, *My Lemonade Stand*. Refer to pages 158–159 for options on how to attach the text.

Assessment

- Have students review the information listed under each flap. On the Student Output page, have them write about what is unique about income and profit. Then, have students write on what the two terms have in common. Provide sentence stems, if needed.

My Lemonade Stand

How It Started

I wanted to buy a bike during summer break. But I had no money. Dad said he had a lemonade stand when he was a kid. It sounded like a fun idea!

Day 1: My First Sale

Dad helped with the shopping. He even lent me the money to pay for everything. It cost $54.00. I will pay him back when I sell some lemonade. I made some lemonade and set up the stand. I charged $1.00 for a cup of lemonade. Mr. Ling was my first customer. He liked the lemonade so much that he bought a second cup!

Today was great! I sold 70 cups and got $70.00! Dad says that is called my *income*. Now, I need to subtract my costs. I spent $54.00 at the store. What is leftover is my *profit*. That can go toward my bike!

Day 2: Ice

If I use ice, the drinks will stay cooler. Also, it takes less lemonade to fill each cup. I will add some ice to Mom's recipe. This means I get 18 cups instead of 12 per batch. So I will earn more money!

The ice worked. I had 50 cups of lemonade leftover from yesterday. With ice, I stretched them to 75 cups. And I sold out. That is $75.00! Dad went to the store for more cups. I had to spend money to pay for the cups. But I still made a profit.

My Lemonade Stand *(cont.)*

Day 3: Jill Murray

I bought more stuff and made more lemonade. But now Jill Murray from school has her own lemonade stand. She will ruin my business! I made some flyers. I asked Mike, my brother, to hand them out to people.

Jill Murray ruined my sales. I only sold 30 cups. That is less than half of what I sold yesterday. But I have spent more money making more lemonade! I spent $66.00 on supplies. I also gave Mike $5.00 for helping with the flyers. Plus, all my ice melted. I won't be able to stretch the lemonade out again. What am I going to do?

Day 4: My Secret Weapon

I had a great idea! I found a recipe on the Internet for blue lemonade. I added $5.00 worth of frozen blueberries to my original recipe. And this was the result: a sellout! I had 120 cups leftover from yesterday. The blueberries stretched that to 135 cups. But I spent $5.00 on blueberries. $135.00 earned – $5.00 spent = $130.00 profit!

My Lemonade Stand Word Web

Directions: Place one letter in each cloud. Write words or phrases that describe, define, or give examples of the words in the center. The words or phrases you write should start with the letters in the clouds.

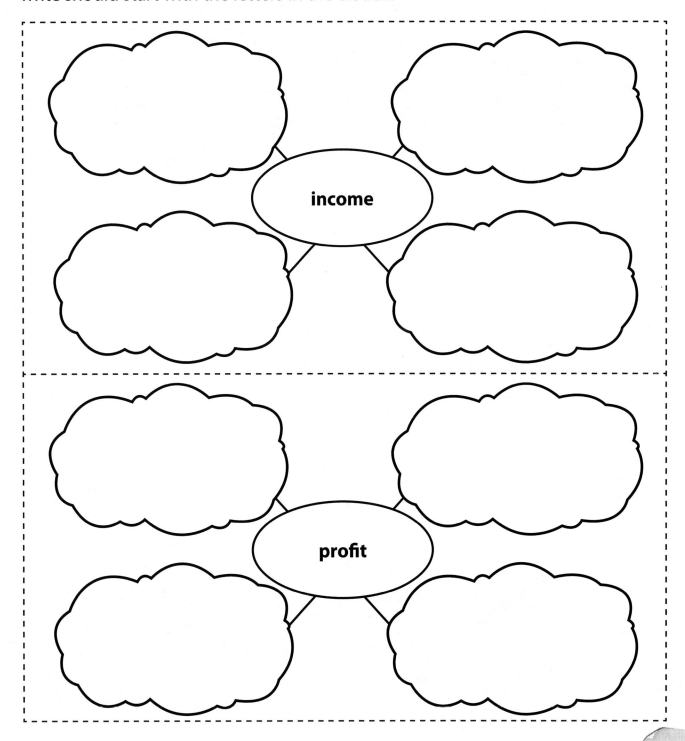

My Lemonade Stand Summary Wheel

Directions: Record details from each section of the text in the Summary Wheel.

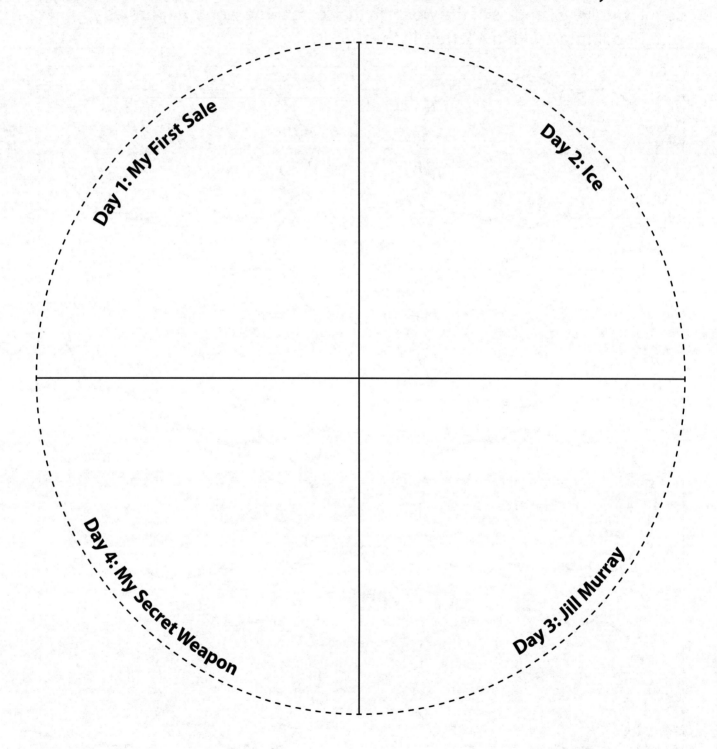

My Lemonade Stand Compare and Contrast

Directions: Cut out the graphic organizer. Fold it in half along the vertical line. Then, cut along the two horizontal lines. Be sure not to cut past the fold. Fold the flaps over.

Basketball Angles

Standards

→ **Mathematics**

Draw and identify lines and angles, and classify shapes by properties of their lines and angles.

→ **Reading**

Read and comprehend complex literary and informational texts independently and proficiently.

→ **Writing**

Produce clear and coherent writing in which the development, organization, and style are appropriate to task, purpose, and audience.

Materials

- copies of *Basketball Angles* (pages 57–58)

- copies of *Basketball Angles KWL Chart* (page 59)

- copies of *Basketball Angles Chart and Match* (page 60)

- index cards (optional)

- sticky notes (different colors if possible; several per student)

- markers, scissors, and glue (or stapler)

- each student's interactive notebook

Graphic Organizer Examples

Before Reading— KWL

During Reading— Chart and Match

After Reading— Stop and Think

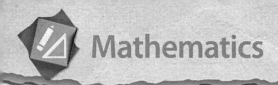

Basketball Angles (cont.)

Before Reading Procedure

Strategy: KWL

1. Distribute copies of *Basketball Angles KWL Chart* (page 59) to students.

2. Tell students that angles are relevant to sports, such as basketball and baseball. Before you discuss the topic with students, brainstorm what they know about angles. You may want to create a list on the board. Ask probing questions to activate prior knowledge.

3. Encourage students to make connections between the information and their prior experiences. You can also give students the option to find partners and discuss what they already know about angles.

4. Have students record their ideas in the *K* section of the *Basketball Angles KWL Chart*. Model how to record ideas in the *K* section. Encourage students to draw pictures if needed.

5. Distribute copies of *Basketball Angles* (pages 57–58) to students. Preview the text with students by skimming for key vocabulary words and text features such as subheadings, boldfaced words, captions, images, or illustrations.

6. Encourage students to discuss anything they may wonder about or want to find out more about through reading or additional research. Students can then meet with partners to discuss the questions they have about the topic.

7. Tell students to record their questions in the *W* section of the activity sheet. Model how to record ideas in the *W* section, if necessary.

   - **Differentiation:** Help students form questions by providing question words such as *Who, What, When, Where, Why,* and *How* on index cards. Have students choose one of the question words, write it in the *W* section, and share their questions either with partners or with the class.

8. Tell students they will read the text later to complete their charts.

Assessment

- On the Student Output page, have students summarize what they think they will learn from the text based on their prior knowledge and what they observed when they previewed it.

During Reading Procedure

Strategy: Chart and Match

1. Write the following words on the board: *acute angle, obtuse angle, right angle, straight angle* and *release point*. Tell students that as they encounter those words in the text, they should highlight, underline, or circle them.

2. Distribute copies of *Basketball Angles Chart and Match* (page 60) to students. Ask them to write the first four vocabulary words in the first column.

3. Tell students to complete the second column by drawing an illustration of each vocabulary word or by giving an example.

Basketball Angles (cont.)

4. Have students complete the third column by reading the context around each vocabulary word and then writing their own definitions.
   - **Differentiation:** To support students in writing their own definitions, provide a variety of sentence stems. For example, *The angle that is less than…; The angle that is more than…; The angle that two line segments or rays meet to form perpendicular lines is….* You may also choose to provide a word bank.

5. After reading the last section of the text, Shoot!, add the final vocabulary term, *release point*, to the chart. Tell students to fill in the second column by writing or drawing examples of the term *release point*. Students should then complete the chart by writing their definitions in the third column. Then, have students cut apart the squares.

6. Have students walk around the room with their pieces and find other students to trade squares with. Explain that when they find a classmate, they should only swap like squares. Students should explain to each partner how they created their definitions and illustrations for the word they are trading. At the end of the activity, each student should end up with a complete chart.

7. Have students create new charts with their new rows on the next Lesson Input page. Students should not glue anything to the page until you have checked their new charts for accuracy.

8. Have students label the three columns with the same terms used on the *Basketball Angles Chart and Match* activity sheet (Vocabulary Word, Illustration/Example, and Definition).

9. Tell students to write the main topic, *Basketball Angles*, at the top of the page above the chart.

10. Have students meet with partners to revisit their KWL charts from the Before Reading activity. Have partners discuss what they learned from the text and whether any of their questions were answered. Have them record this in the *L* section. Have students add any additional questions they have about the text to the *W* section.

11. After students have completed their KWL charts, ask them to fold the right and left sides of the KWL chart into the center so that they cover the *W* section. Have them put glue on the back of the *W* section and attach the KWL chart to the next Lesson Input page.

Assessment

- On the Student Output page, ask each student to choose one of the vocabulary words and write it at the top of the page. Then, have them write a few sentences to relate it to their own experiences.

After Reading Procedure

Strategy: Stop and Think

1. Distribute 12 sticky notes to each student. If possible, provide students with three different colors.

2. Review the text together, explaining that it is a nonfiction article. Then, explain that the text is broken into four sections: About Angles, Dribbling, Make the Pass, and Shoot! Reread the text with students. If possible, project the text on the board with the sections numbered so that students can refer to it as they read.

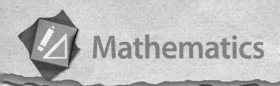

Basketball Angles *(cont.)*

3. Tell students to turn to the next Lesson Input page and title it *Stop and Think*. Directly under the strategy title, have students write the title of the text, "Basketball Angles."

4. Have students spread out the sticky notes on their desks. Tell each student to write exclamation points on three sticky notes, stars on three, and question marks on three. Explain what each symbol means:

   - **!** I find this interesting.

   - **✳** I can explain this.

   - **?** I have a question about this.

5. Begin with the About Angles section of the text. Read the section together, and discuss the process of placing sticky notes beside sentences. For example, you might place the exclamation point beside the sentence, "A straight angle, or line, measures 180 degrees." Explain that you find this interesting because you did not realize that a straight line was a type of angle. Have each student underline a sentence he or she found interesting and place the exclamation point beside it.
   - **Differentiation:** Draw a line between each section to show students when they should stop and think.

6. Repeat this process with the other two sticky notes. After finishing all three sticky notes in the first section, provide students time to share where they placed their sticky notes.

7. Tell students to write about the parts of the text that they flagged. First, model writing the section title, About Angles, at the top of the page.

8. Model how to remove each sticky note from the text and transfer it to the notes page below the About Angles heading. As you remove each sticky note, write the information that you flagged in the right section of the notes page. Conclude by reviewing your notes.

9. Tell students to continue the Stop and Think process with the other three sections of text, using additional sticky notes.
   - **Differentiation:** For students who complete the task early or need an additional challenge, encourage them to research the unanswered questions they wrote during the KWL or the Stop and Think sections of the lesson.
   - This activity may run over several Lesson Input pages.

10. Have students turn to the next Lesson Input page and attach the text, *Basketball Angles*. Refer to pages 158–159 for options on how to attach the text.

Assessment

- On the Student Output page, have students use their notes to write or draw summaries about the topic. Encourage students to include vocabulary words from the text. Have students circle any questions that were not answered in the text and include statements that explain how this strategy helps them understand the content.

Basketball Angles

About Angles

There are different categories of angles. An acute angle is less than 90°. An obtuse angle is larger than 90° but is less than 180°. A right angle measures exactly 90°, and the two line segments or rays that meet at a right angle are said to be perpendicular. A straight angle, or line, measures 180°.

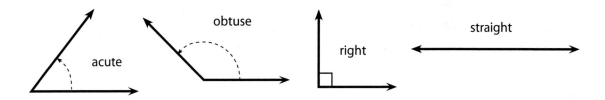

Dribbling

Angles can be found in basketball. Passing the basketball is the quickest way to move it up the court, but you may need to dribble it until you can make a good pass to someone on your team. Sometimes, opposing players will guard you closely; keep your hand on top of the ball as you dribble in this situation. This makes your dribble low and the angle perpendicular to the ground. This will make it hard for the opposition to steal the ball. If you are not tightly guarded, you can go for speed when dribbling. Place your hand behind the ball at an acute angle. Your hand should be about 90° away from your body. Then, push the ball hard and fast in front of you, below your hip level.

Make the Pass

Good passing will help you win basketball games. If there is no defender between you and a teammate, you can make a two-handed chest pass. Hold the ball in two hands at about chest height, close to your body. Spread your fingers and keep your thumbs and wrists at an upward angle. Then, step in the direction of your pass for extra power and speed. Release the ball with a snap of your wrist, which will help the ball travel in a straight angle to your teammate.

Basketball Angles *(cont.)*

If there is a defender, make a two-handed bounce pass. Hold the ball as you would for a chest pass and step forward as you throw. Put spin on the ball by positioning your thumbs down as you release it. The ball should hit the floor at least three-quarters of the way between you and your teammate. It will bounce at an angle and arrive around your teammate's thigh and waist area for an easy catch.

Shoot!

Angle is important when shooting baskets. Whether a ball goes into the basket depends on the angle. When a basketball shooter lets go of the ball, this is called the *release point*. It is best to have a high release point when aiming for the hoop. A low release point means the ball will go through the basket at a low angle, around 30° to 50°. The ball is less likely to go through the hoop at this angle. You have a higher chance of making a basket if you have a high release point. This increases the angle that the ball enters the hoop. So a basketball that drops toward the basket at a 70° to 90° angle from above has a larger target to enter.

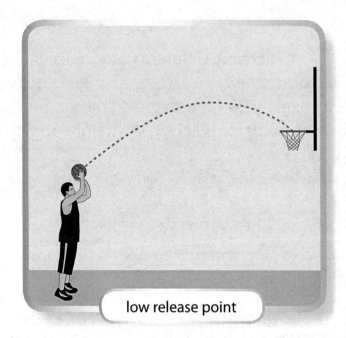

low release point

high release point

Basketball Angles KWL Chart

Directions: Use the chart to help you brainstorm what you know (*K*), want to know (*W*), and learned about a topic (*L*).

Topic: _____

What You KNOW

What You WANT to Know

What You LEARNED

Name: _____ Date:_____

Basketball Angles Chart and Match

Directions: Write the vocabulary words in the first column. Draw an illustration or give an example of the word in the second column. Write your own definition in the third column.

Vocabulary Word	Illustration/Example	Definition

51733—Interactive Notetaking for Content-Area Literacy

Patterns Around Us

Standards

→ **Mathematics**

Generate a number or shape pattern that follows a given rule. Identify apparent features of the pattern that were not explicit in the rule itself.

→ **Reading**

Interpret words and phrases as they are used in a text, including determining technical, connotative, and figurative meanings, and analyze how specific word choices shape meaning or tone.

→ **Writing**

Produce clear and coherent writing in which the development, organization, and style are appropriate to task, purpose, and audience.

Materials

- copies of *Patterns Around Us* (pages 65–66)

- copies of *Patterns Around Us Clock Partners* (page 67) (optional)

- copies of *Patterns Around Us Reading-Review Web* (page 68) (optional)

- uncoated paper plates (1 per student)

- sticky notes (4 per student)

- 8.5" x 11" sheets of colored paper (1 per student)

- index cards (8 per student)

- 10-inch sealed envelopes (2 per student)

- markers, scissors, and glue (or stapler)

- each student's interactive notebook

Graphic Organizer Examples

Before Reading—Clock Partners

During Reading—Pocket It!

After Reading—Reading-Review Web

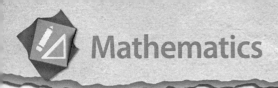

Patterns Around Us *(cont.)*

Before Reading Procedure

Strategy: Clock Partners

1. Distribute a paper plate and four sticky notes to each student. Have students write their names in the centers of their paper plates. Model how to label the hours of the clock (1 through 12) around the edges of their plates. Then, draw lines from the center of the plate to each of the 12 hours where students will write their names. Then, have students create their own plates following your modeled example.
   - **Differentiation:** Limit the number of hours put on the clock at one time. Start with only four hours, and then add the others a few days later.
   - In place of creating this on paper plates, you may choose to distribute copies of *Patterns Around Us Clock Partners* (page 67) to students.

2. Have students find one classmate for each labeled hour. When they find partners, have them write each other's names beside the same hour. For example, Meghan partners with Rassoul. They both write each other's names in the 5:00 spot. Remind students that they must each find a different partner for each hour and that all of their hours must be filled. Provide a few minutes for students to find partners.
   - **Differentiation:** Model how to find partners by choosing a student "partner" and acting out the process of "scheduling" a time slot. Repeat the process of writing each other's names a couple of times before encouraging students to continue on their own.

3. Once students have found their partners, have them attach their completed paper plates (or copies of completed page 67) onto an empty Lesson Input page.

4. Distribute copies of *Patterns Around Us* (pages 65–66) to students. Tell them that they will meet with their 1:00 partner to preview the text. Explain that they should highlight the title and the subtitles.

5. Have students meet with different clock partners to skim the text. Tell students to circle or underline any boldfaced or italicized words in the text.

6. Ask students to meet with other clock partners to skim the text more closely and create a question for the first section, Patterns in Nature. They should each write a question on a sticky note. For example, they may notice the word *camouflage* and ask the question, *What does camouflage have to do with patterns and animals?*

7. Call out another clock partner, and repeat Step 6 for the remaining sections, Geometric Patterns and Number Patterns.

8. Tell students to glue their sticky-note questions onto the next Student Output page. Then, have them share some of the questions they wrote with the rest of the class. As students continue to read the text more closely, they should look for answers to their questions. If they find answers to their own questions, have them jot down the answers on the Student Output page next to their sticky notes.

Patterns Around Us *(cont.)*

Assessment

- During the conversations between clock partners, listen for words such as *camouflage*, *strata*, *transformation*, and *tessellations*.

- On the Student Output page, ask students to write any answers they found to their questions. Monitor the pages to see if students are successfully answering their own questions.

During Reading Procedure

Strategy: Pocket It!

1. Tell students to read the text either independently or with partners.

2. Write the following words from the text on the board: *strata*, *transformation*, and *tessellations*. Have each student choose one other word they would like to learn more about. As they read, have them circle or underline those words as well as any context clues surrounding them.

3. Distribute two sealed envelopes to each student. Have students hold the envelopes vertically, fold them in half using a horizontal fold, and crease the fold.

4. Model how to cut the envelope into two halves by cutting along the creased fold. By cutting the fold, they should create two pockets. Have students repeat these steps with the next envelope.

5. Have students write the word *strata* on the first pocket, *transformation* on the second pocket, *tessellations* on the third pocket, and their chosen word on the last pocket.

6. Distribute eight index cards to each student. Reread the text as a class, or have students read the text independently. Students should focus on the context surrounding the four vocabulary words they annotated in Step 2.
   - You may need to model this initially. For example, reread the third paragraph in the section Patterns in Nature. Draw students' attention to instances of the word *strata*. Discuss what the text says about *strata* to brainstorm a possible definition. A good definition might be *the layers of rock that have built up over millions of years*.

7. Have each student write the definition of *strata* on an index card. Then, have them follow the same process for the words *transformation*, *tessellations*, and the words they chose. After students have completed their definitions, they should each have four blank index cards. Have students draw illustrations or examples that describe each vocabulary word on the remaining index cards.
   - **Differentiation:** Work with a small group of below-level learners to complete the definitions. Model how to think about the meaning of a word by studying the context around it. Show students additional strategies to assist them, such as jotting down the definitions in the margins before writing it on the index cards.

8. Have students place their definition and illustration/example cards in the pockets that match each vocabulary word. Then, tell them to glue two pockets onto the next Student Output page and two pockets onto the following Student Output page.

9. Tell students to use their vocabulary cards to quiz their 9:00 clock partners.

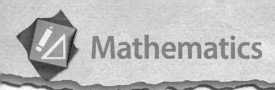
Patterns Around Us (cont.)

Assessment

- Observe students as they quiz one another. Determine whether students can successfully match the definitions and the illustrations/examples with the vocabulary words.

- Have students work with partners to have discussions using the vocabulary words. Explain that their conversations should combine what they know about "Patterns Around Us" and what they know about patterns around them in their everyday lives.

After Reading Procedure

Strategy: Reading-Review Web

1. Distribute an 8.5" x 11" sheet of colored paper and a sticky note to each student. Have students fold their papers horizontally, and then fold them in half vertically. When opened, each paper should have four equal sections.
   - In place of using separate colored paper, you may choose to distribute copies of *Patterns Around Us Reading-Review Web* (page 68) to students.

2. Have each student place a sticky note in the center of the folded paper and title it *Patterns Around Us*. Then, ask students to label each of the four sections *Supporting Detail*.

3. Explain that students should review the sections of the text and consider the images they create in their minds as they read. They should then draw or write about those images in the four *Supporting Detail* boxes. The drawings or explanations should represent details that support the main idea.
   - **Differentiation:** Challenge above-level learners to also include one or two examples of details from the text that do not specifically support the main idea but are interesting or informative.

4. Once students have completed their review webs, have them meet with their 12:00 clock partners (chosen in the Before Reading section), and discuss the supporting details for the text, *Patterns Around Us*.

5. After talking with their partners, tell students to make any revisions needed on their review webs to make the webs more detailed. Then, have students fold their papers over the horizontal fold again and glue them onto the next Lesson Input page.

6. Have students turn to the next Lesson Input page and attach the text, *Patterns Around Us*. Refer to pages 158–159 for options on how to attach the text.

Assessment

- Encourage students to consider how visualizing the text while they read helps them draw images to represent the main idea and supporting details. On the Student Output page, have students write about patterns they notice in their own world.

- Have students who need a challenge create complex patterns of their own, draw them on the Student Output page, and explain the patterns in their own words.

Patterns Around Us

Patterns in Nature

There are many patterns in nature. Plants are known by their leaf shapes and by the vein patterns on their leaves. Look at some leaves. The patterns are different for each kind of tree. Even flower petals are in patterns. Daisies have long, narrow petals that form circles.

Many animals have patterns on their bodies. Bees have striped patterns. Butterflies and moths have patterns on their wings. Leopards have spotted patterns. Their spots are used as camouflage in the long grass. Zebras have black and white stripes. Zebras can recognize one another. The striped patterns are different on each animal!

Rocks often show patterns. Layers of rock build up over millions of years. These layers are called *strata*. The pattern of the different strata can be seen on cliff faces. At the Grand Canyon in Arizona, you can see many layers of strata. Each layer of rock is its own color. The layers form striped patterns on the cliff faces. Scientists study these patterns. Some layers show that the area was once a shallow sea. Other layers show that the area was a swamp or a desert.

Geometric Patterns

Geometric patterns are easy to make. Repeating just one shape makes a simple pattern. You can make the pattern look different by changing colors. You can also use different shapes. You can even change the positions of the shapes by flipping or turning them. This is called *transformation*. Transforming a shape, such as turning or flipping it, makes a more complex pattern. Turning, or rotating, a shape makes another pattern.

Patterns Around Us *(cont.)*

tessellation

People have used tiles to make patterns for thousands of years. These patterns are called *tessellations*. A tessellation is a pattern that covers a space. There are no overlaps or gaps between the shapes. Polygons are used for these types of patterns. Squares, triangles, and hexagons fit neatly together by themselves in tessellations. Circles will not fit the pattern unless other shapes are added to fill the gaps. In some tessellations, the patterns are inside a shape, such as a square. This is repeated over and over again. Other tessellations have symmetrical patterns.

Number Patterns

Our system of numbers is based on patterns in groups of 10. We count from 1 to 10 and then repeat the numbers in more sets of 10. Then we count in sets of 100, then sets of 1,000, and so on. No matter how far we count, the same pattern of numbers keeps going. We can see many patterns in a grid of 100 numbers. If we count by 10s, we get a vertical pattern on the grid. Counting by 9s makes a diagonal pattern.

Numbers make many patterns. It is easy to multiply by 9s if you know there is a pattern. The number in the 10s column is always 1 less than the number you are multiplying by. And the sum of the numbers always adds up to 9.

Name: _____ Date:_____

Patterns Around Us Clock Partners

Directions: Write a partner's name for each hour. You should have 12 different partners when you are finished.

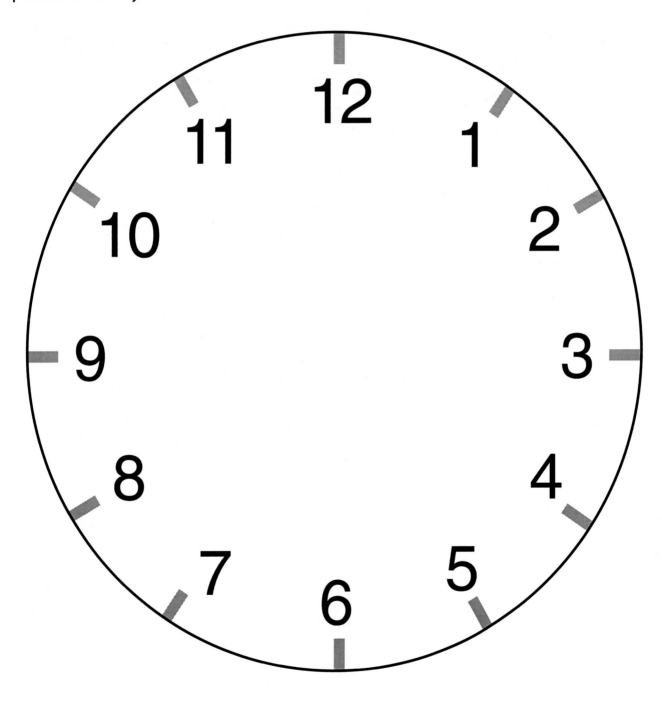

Name: _____ Date: _____

Patterns Around Us Reading-Review Web

Directions: Review the sections of the text. As you read, create images in your mind about the main idea. Then, draw or write details that support the main idea.

Supporting Detail

Supporting Detail

Patterns Around Us

Supporting Detail

Supporting Detail

States of Matter

Standards

→ **Science**

Understands the structure and properties of matter.

→ **Reading**

Interpret words and phrases as they are used in a text, including determining technical, connotative, and figurative meanings, and analyze how specific word choices shape meaning or tone.

→ **Writing**

Produce clear and coherent writing in which the development, organization, and style are appropriate to task, purpose, and audience.

Materials

- copies of *States of Matter* (pages 73–74)

- copies of *States of Matter Think-Pair-Square-Share* (page 75)

- copies of *States of Matter Frayer Model* (3 per student) (page 76) (optional)

- copies of *States of Matter Three-Sides Notetaking* (page 77)

- poster chart (1 per group; optional)

- 8.5" x 11" sheets of paper (different colors if possible; 3 per student)

- markers, scissors, and glue (or stapler)

- each student's interactive notebook

Graphic Organizer Examples

Before Reading— Think-Pair-Square-Share

During Reading— Frayer Model

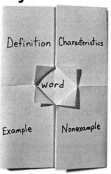

After Reading— Three-Sides Notetaking

States of Matter *(cont.)*

Before Reading Procedure

Strategy: Think-Pair-Square-Share

1. Distribute copies of *States of Matter Think-Pair-Square-Share* (page 75) to students. Project the word *matter* for students. Ask students to think about the word as it relates to science.

2. Ask students to think about the question, *What are the states of matter and the unique properties of each?* Have students record their answers in the *Think* box on the activity sheet.
   - **Differentiation:** Display pictures of objects that portray the three states of matter. Encourage students to observe the pictures and find similarities in the properties of the objects.

3. Tell each student to share their answers with the person next to them. Pairs of students should collaborate to find the best answer to share with other classmates and an explanation of why each is the best. Then, have each pair write their answer and explanation in the *Pair* box on the activity sheet.

4. Have students share their answers in groups of four or more, depending on class size. Have each pair share their answers with the group.

5. Each group should decide which answer they think is best as well as an explanation of their reasoning. Once an answer has been agreed upon, students should write their group's answer and the justification in the *Square* box on the activity sheet.
   - **Differentiation:** Once the Square groups have agreed upon their best answers to share with the class, ask students to transfer their group answers to a poster chart. Each group could then present its answer to the rest of the class. You may choose for the class to do a gallery walk so they can get a closer look at each group's presentation.

6. Ask students to share their group choices and reasoning with the class. Have students write the best answers they heard along with explanations defending their choices in the *Share* box on the activity sheet.

7. Have students fold their activity sheets into quarters. Tell them to glue the bottom-right quarter of their completed *States of Matter Think-Pair-Square-Share* activity sheets onto an empty Lesson Input page.

8. On the Student Output page, have students write summaries of their discussions. Tell students to include their final answers and why they chose them.

Assessment

- On the Student Output page, students should compose single paragraphs that express their final answers. Explain that students will use the notes they took from the various groups and compile a cohesive paragraph. Remind students that this final step should explain, in detail, their final answers.

States of Matter (cont.)

During Reading Procedure

Strategy: Frayer Model

1. Distribute copies of *States of Matter* (pages 73–74) to students. Have them read the text in pairs.

2. Ask students to annotate the text by circling the three states of matter and underlining the unique properties of each. As they read, they should write examples of each state of matter in the margins. For example, a student circles the word *solids* and underlines the properties (hard or soft, big or small). They might write *plastic*, *metal*, *stone*, *bone*, *straw*, *sand*, *crackers*, or *ice* in the margin.

3. Distribute three 8.5" x 11" sheets of different colored paper to each student. Tell students to fold the first sheet of paper horizontally.
   - You may choose to distribute three copies of *States of Matter Frayer Model* (page 76) to students instead of blank paper. Have students cut out the template and continue with the steps below.

4. Have students open the folded paper and hold it in landscape layout. Then, tell them to fold each edge of the paper to the creased fold to create a "shutter-doors" fold.

5. While the "shutter doors" are still folded inward, have students cut both the doors in half horizontally to create four flaps. Monitor students closely as they complete this step to ensure that they cut correctly.

6. While still folded, have each student flip up the four center corners of the flaps to create a diamond-shaped window in the center of their paper. Tell students to write the word *solids* in their windows.

7. While the flaps are still closed, have students label the flaps.
   - top left: *Definition*
   - top right: *Characteristics*
   - bottom left: *Example*
   - bottom right: *Non-Example*

8. Talk through an example of how to complete the template using the term *solids*.
   - **Differentiation:** To assist students in completing their booklets, provide sentence stems, such as *Some examples of solids are….*

9. Have students repeat Steps 3–7 to create Frayer model booklets for the other two states of matter.

10. Have students fold their Frayer model booklets back over the horizontal folds from Step 3. Then, tell them to put the books in alphabetical order. Next, have students number the booklets 1–3 from left to right.

11. Show students how to stack the booklets one on top of the other so all the folds are on the left and all the open ends are on the right. Booklet 1 should be on top, followed by booklets 2 and 3. Have students attach the booklets together by gluing one on top of the other.

12. Have students write the title, *States of Matter*, on the front cover of the stacked booklets. Students can then attach the booklets onto the next Lesson Input page.

States of Matter *(cont.)*

Assessment

- On the Student Output page, have students draw three columns and label them *Solids*, *Liquids*, and *Gases*. In each column, they should write things in their everyday lives that have the correct properties. For example, under the *Liquids* column, students may write *water*.

After Reading Procedure

Strategy: Three-Sides Notetaking

1. Distribute copies of *States of Matter Three-Sides Notetaking* (page 77) to students. Have them cut along the outer edges of the square.

2. Draw students' attention to the four triangles that make up the square. Explain that they will be using the top, bottom, and right triangles for notetaking. The triangle labeled *glue* should not be written on.

3. Have students refer to the annotations they made while reading the text. Tell students to record notes about each state of matter on their templates as they reread. Depending on students' ability levels, you may choose to model this. Some examples you could write to describe solids are *hard*, *soft*, *computers*, or *ice*.
   - **Differentiation:** Create a word bank of adjectives students can reference when describing the states of matter. If needed, students can create picture cards to help explain the different adjectives in the word bank.

4. After students have completed their notes, have them cut along the dashed lines. Monitor to ensure that they stop in the center of the square and do not cut on the solid line beyond the cut line.

5. Have students make folds on the solid lines. Students should then put small amounts of glue on the triangle labeled *glue*. Tell students to move the bottom triangle up and over the glue section. The bottom triangle should overlap and cover the glue section. Then, students can press down lightly to adhere the glue. Students should now have three-dimensional notes pages.

6. Have students glue their triangular prisms onto the next Lesson Input page. They should glue only the bottom section of the triangle to the notebook. Additionally, tell students to title the page *States of Matter*. Have students fold the triangular shapes so they lay flat.

7. Have students turn to the next Lesson Input page and attach the text, *States of Matter*. Refer to pages 158–159 for options on how to attach the text.

Assessment

- Tell each student to think about the text and the notes he or she took on the template. On their Student Output pages, have students write haikus to describe one of the states of matter. A haiku is a three-line poem. The first line has five syllables, the second line has seven syllables, and the third line has five lines. Have students illustrate their haikus.

States of Matter

Matter can take the form of a solid, a liquid, or a gas. Each state of matter has its own unique set of properties.

Solids

Solids can be hard or soft, or they can be big or small. Wood is one example of solid matter. Plastic, metal, stone, bone, straw, sand, and crackers are all solids. Human-made solids include everything from computers to keys to the clothes you wear. Ice, the solid state of water, is a familiar solid. Objects in a solid state don't change shape easily.

Liquids

Unlike solids, liquids do change shape. They can flow, pour, and even be spilled. They change their shape to fill any space around them. Milk, oil, and ink are all liquids. Have you ever accidentally knocked over a cup of juice? Most likely, the juice came flowing out of the cup and spilled all over the place. It may have run off the table and onto the floor. This is because liquid flows freely unless it is stopped by a container or barrier. Water is the most common liquid found on Earth. It doesn't have a definite, stable shape as ice has. Instead, when it is located inside of something, it takes the shape of that container. If there isn't a container, water continues flowing, just like the spilled juice. Water is made of the same molecules found in ice but the molecules in water move more freely, while the molecules in ice move minimally.

States of Matter *(cont.)*

Gases

Gases don't have any shapes or sizes of their own. They spread quickly to fill the spaces around them. Similar to liquids, gases flow easily. But they can also be compressed, or squeezed. One example of compression is shown in a basketball. Gas is forced into a small hole in the ball with an inflator needle. When the needle is removed, the hole closes—gas can only escape if the hole opens. Gases are often invisible. So, most of the time, we cannot see them. But gases are all around you; even an empty glass is filled with air. The air we breathe in is a mixture of multiple gases, including oxygen.

States of Matter Think-Pair-Square-Share

Directions: Complete the table with information from the text.

Think 	Pair
Think of your answer. Write or draw your answer.	Talk with your partner. Write or draw your answer.
Square	**Share**
Meet with your group. Write or draw the best answer.	Listen to the groups. Decide on the best answer. Write or draw this answer.

Name: _____ Date:_____

States of Matter Frayer Model

Directions: Cut along the dashed lines, and fold along the solid lines to create your template.

Example	**Non-Example**

Definition	**Characteristics**

51733—Interactive Notetaking for Content-Area Literacy © Shell Education

States of Matter Three-Sides Notetaking

Directions: Cut along the outer edges of the square. Record notes about each state of matter under the correct flap. Then, cut along the dashed line. Do not cut on the solid lines.

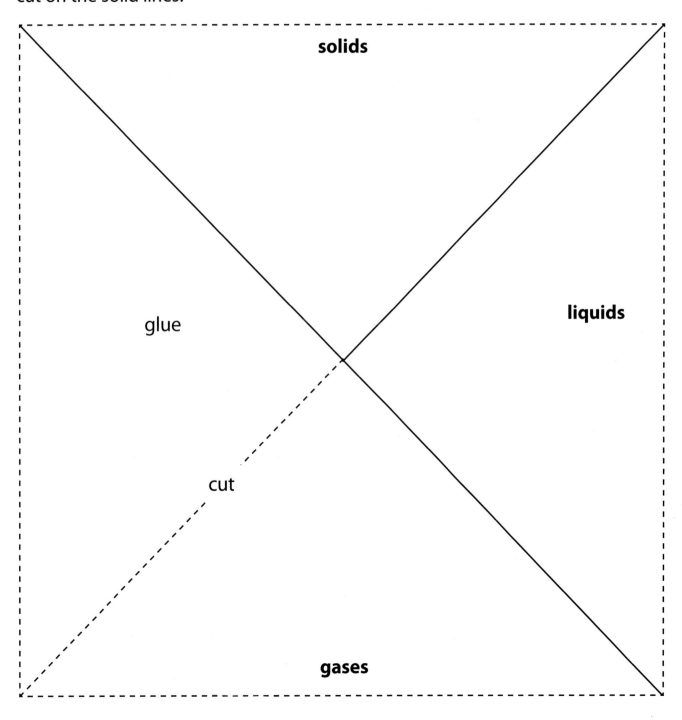

solids

glue

liquids

cut

gases

The Water Cycle

Standards

➠ **Science**

Understands atmospheric processes and the water cycle.

➠ **Reading**

Interpret words and phrases as they are used in a text, including determining technical, connotative, and figurative meanings, and analyze how specific word choices shape meaning or tone.

➠ **Writing**

Write informative/explanatory texts to examine and convey complex ideas and information clearly and accurately through the effective selection, organization, and analysis of content.

Materials

- copies of *The Water Cycle* (pages 83–84)
- copies of *The Water Cycle Find Your Corner* (page 85) (optional)
- copies of *The Water Cycle Four-Triangle Notetaking* (page 86) (optional)
- copies of *The Water Cycle Fact or Fib* (page 87) (optional)
- 4 large poster charts
- 8.5" x 11" sheets of colored paper (1 per student)
- index cards (3–5 per student)
- 10-inch sealed envelope (1 per 2 students)
- markers, scissors, and glue (or stapler)
- each student's interactive notebook

Graphic Organizer Examples

Before Reading— Find Your Corner

During Reading— Four-Triangle Notetaking

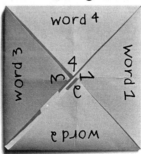

After Reading— Fact or Fib

The Water Cycle *(cont.)*

Before Reading Procedure

Strategy: Find Your Corner

1. Before beginning the lesson, write each of the following sentence stems on one of the posters: *I am brand new…*; *I know a little…*; *I know more than a little, but I am not an expert…*; and *I am an expert….* Hang one poster in each of the four corners of the room.

2. Have students turn to the next Lesson Input page. Ask each student to draw a vertical line down the center of the page and a horizontal line across the center of the page.
   - In place of creating this directly in the notebooks, you may choose to distribute copies of *The Water Cycle Find Your Corner* (page 85) to students. Have them cut out the table at the end of the activity and glue it onto the Lesson Input page.

3. Draw students' attention to the four posters. Ask them to label each square on their page to match each poster.

4. Introduce the topic of the water cycle. Depending on students' level of knowledge, you could have a brief discussion about the water cycle. You may also choose to display some pictures of the different steps or preview the text with students. Provide students time to think about the topic.

5. Ask each student to decide which poster applies to his or her level of prior knowledge. Once students have decided, they should each justify why they chose their level by writing notes in the correct corner of the graphic organizer. For example, if a student knows a couple parts of the water cycle, he or she should write a couple of bullet points about the water cycle in the *I know a little…* section.

- **Differentiation:** Provide students with sentence stems to help them describe their prior knowledge about the water cycle. For students who struggle with basic vocabulary, provide a word bank to help them complete the sentences.

6. Tell students to move to the corner of the room with the poster that matches their levels of prior knowledge. Students should bring their notebooks with them. Then, have students discuss with their poster groups why they each chose that poster.

7. After the group discussion, have students return to their desks. Tell them to attach their graphic organizers onto the next Lesson Input page. Tell students that they will refer back to this graphic organizer at the end of the lesson.

Assessment

- On the Student Output page, have students write a few sentences on what they have learned about the water cycle.

During Reading Procedure

Strategy: Four-Triangle Notetaking

1. Distribute copies of *The Water Cycle* (pages 83–84) to students. Tell them that they will organize information to explain their understandings of the water cycle. Have them read the text with partners. Tell students to highlight and/or annotate the important information for each of the steps in the text.

The Water Cycle (cont.)

2. Distribute an 8.5" x 11" sheet of colored paper to each student. Have students fold one of the corners to the opposite side to form a right triangle. Students should cut off the remaining strip of paper. When the fold is opened, the paper should be a square.
   - In place of creating this on blank sheets of paper, you may choose to distribute copies of *The Water Cycle Four-Triangle Notetaking* (page 86) to students. Have them cut out this page and fold as directed to create their graphic organizers.

3. Tell students to fold the square in half to create another diagonal fold perpendicular to the first fold. Next, have students fold the corners into the center of the square where all the folds meet. This will create the four-triangle graphic organizer. Have students number the triangles *1, 2, 3,* and *4.*

4. Ask students to label the outside of the first triangle *Evaporation*, the second triangle *Condensation*, the third triangle *Precipitation*, and the fourth triangle, *Runoff*. Have students draw an illustration of each step on top of the appropriate triangle.

5. Have students describe each step of the water cycle under each of the four triangles. They should use their annotations from the text to determine the details they want to include.
   - **Differentiation:** Scaffold this activity by changing what information is expected on students' graphic organizers. Or, create a word bank of the key vocabulary words for each of the four steps.

6. Tell students to title the next Lesson Input page, *The Water Cycle*. Have them glue their four-triangle graphic organizers below the title.

Assessment

- Ask students to use their graphic organizers as a prewriting activity for paragraphs that describe the steps of the water cycle. Provide a rubric to identify the expectations for the paragraph, such as paragraphs must include a main idea and details, complete sentences, and key vocabulary.

- Tell students to refer back to their Find Your Corner graphic organizers. Have them reflect on their current level of knowledge about the water cycle.

After Reading Procedure

Strategy: Fact or Fib

1. After students have read *The Water Cycle*, place them into heterogeneous groups of four or five. Assign a section of the text for each group to read and review.

2. Distribute index cards to students. Have each group create two to four fact cards and one fib card for their assigned section of the text. Tell students that although they will choose their facts and fibs as a group, each student will need to make his or her own copy of the group's fact and fib cards.

3. To create the fact cards, ask students to review their sections and write facts on the fronts of their index cards. Tell students to choose facts they think are most important. On the backs of their cards, have students write evidence to support the facts.

The Water Cycle *(cont.)*

4. Model how to create a fib card that is relevant and appropriate for the content, but that is also untrue. Have students write the fibs on the fronts of their last index cards.
   - **Differentiation:** Create several example cards before students begin the activity using the ones provided in *The Water Cycle Fact or Fib* (page 87). Model how to change a fact statement to a fib. Then, have students write the fibs on the backs of the cards and explain how they created the fibs from the facts.

5. Distribute one envelope to every two students. Ask each pair of students to cut it in half horizontally to create two pockets. Each student should take one half and write the title *The Water Cycle* on the envelope. Students should then attach their envelope pockets onto the next Lesson Input page and place the fact or fib cards in the pockets.

6. Explain that you will now jigsaw the groups. Place students into new groups so that each group has a student for every section of the text. The new groups will then take turns using the Fact or Fib cards to quiz each other. (Make sure they mix up their cards before starting so that the fib cards aren't always everyone's last card.)

7. Have students share with their groups the section of text they were responsible for reviewing. Ask them to read their fact or fib statements to the rest of the group. The group will then discuss which of the statements they think are the facts and which statement is a fib. They may use the text to help them. Encourage students to take notes about the group discussion on the Student Output page.

8. Discuss how students' levels of knowledge about the water cycle have increased since the beginning of the lesson.

9. Have students turn to the next Lesson Input page and attach the text, *The Water Cycle*. Refer to pages 158–159 for options on how to attach the text.

Assessment

- On the Student Output page, ask students to write the numbers *3*, *2*, *1* vertically down the page. Next to *3*, have students write three facts they learned about the water cycle. Next to *2*, have them write two facts they found interesting about the water cycle. Next to *1*, have students write one question they have about the water cycle. Provide sentence stems if needed.

51733—Interactive Notetaking for Content-Area Literacy © Shell Education

Name: _____ Date:_____

The Water Cycle

Some things happen over and over. They occur in the same order. This is called a *cycle*. Water moves in a cycle. There are four parts of the water cycle: **evaporation**, **condensation**, **precipitation**, and **runoff**.

The cycle starts when the sun warms the water. The water evaporates. It turns into vapor. Next, the vapor rises into the air. There, it cools and makes clouds. This is condensation.

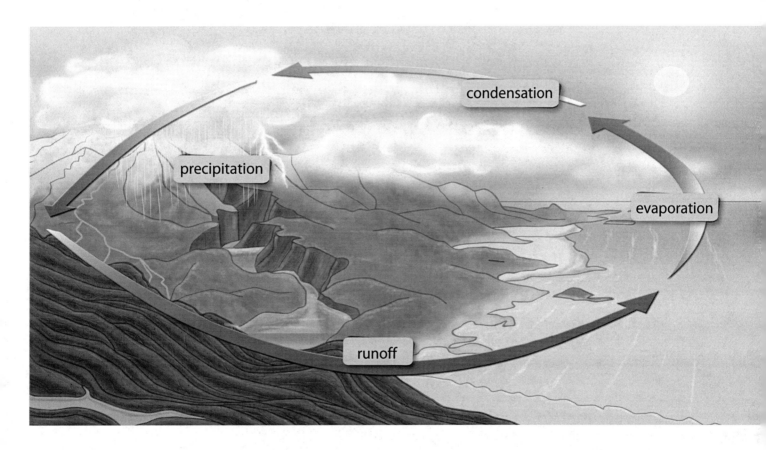

The Water Cycle *(cont.)*

As clouds get colder, tiny drops of water form. Soon the drops fall from the clouds. Sometimes, they fall as rain. Other times, they fall as **hail**. If it is cold enough, they fall as snow! These are all types of precipitation.

The water falls to Earth. It collects in lakes and rivers. It flows to the oceans. This is called runoff. When the water warms up, the cycle starts again!

Each snowflake is unique.

hail

Name: _____ Date:_____

The Water Cycle Find Your Corner

Directions: Decide which corner best describes your prior knowledge of the water cycle. In that corner, write a few sentences explaining why you chose it.

The Water Cycle	
I am brand new…	I am an expert…
I know a little…	I know more than a little, but I am not an expert…

The Water Cycle Four-Triangle Notetaking

Directions: Cut out the square. Fold along the solid lines. Then, fold each corner into the center where the two lines meet.

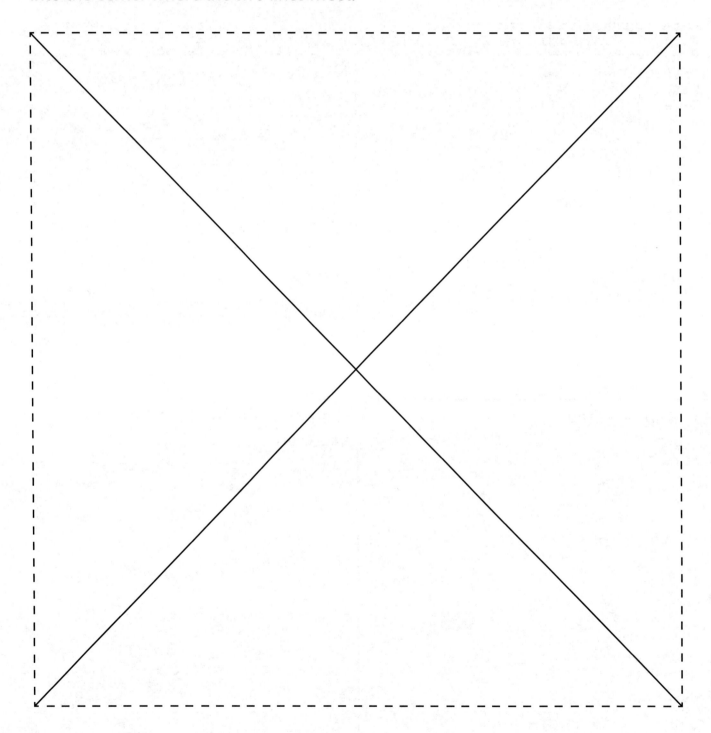

The Water Cycle Fact or Fib

Directions: Cut each card apart. Decide which statements are facts and which are fibs.

Precipitation can fall as rain, snow, or hail.

Water warms up to form clouds.

Water turns to vapor when it evaporates.

Runoff is what happens when water vapor condenses.

The cycle starts over when water warms up again.

Producers and Consumers

Standards

➠ **Science**

Understands relationships among organisms and their physical environment.

➠ **Reading**

Determine central ideas or themes of a text and analyze their development; summarize the key supporting details and ideas.

➠ **Writing**

Write narratives to develop real or imagined experiences or events using effective technique, well-chosen details and well-structured event sequences.

Materials

- copies of *Producers and Consumers* (pages 93–94)

- copies of *Producers and Consumers Peer Partner Review* (page 95)

- copies of *Producers and Consumers Reading-Review Web* (page 96) (optional)

- sticky notes (different colors if possible; several per student)

- 8.5" x 11" sheets of colored paper (2 per student)

- timer

- markers, scissors, and glue (or stapler)

- each student's interactive notebook

Graphic Organizer Examples

Before Reading—Stop and Think

During Reading—Peer Partner Review

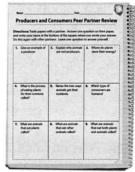

After Reading—Reading-Review Web

Producers and Consumers (cont.)

Before Reading Procedure

Strategy: Stop and Think

1. Distribute nine sticky notes to each student. If possible, provide students with three different colors.

2. Distribute copies of *Producers and Consumers* (pages 93–94) to students. Preview the text together, explaining that this is a nonfiction article.

3. Explain that the text is broken into three sections: Producers, Getting Energy, and Types of Consumers. Preview the three sections. If possible, project the text on the board with the sections numbered so that students can refer to it as they read.

4. Tell students to turn to the next Lesson Input page and title it *Stop and Think*. Directly under the strategy title, have students write the title of the text, *Producers and Consumers*.

5. Ask students to spread out the sticky notes on their desks. Have them write exclamation points on three sticky notes, stars on three, and question marks on three. Explain what each symbol means.

   - **!** I find this interesting.

   - **★** I can explain this.

   - **?** I have a question about this.

6. Begin with the Producers section of the text. Skim the text together, and discuss the process of placing sticky notes beside sentences. Tell students that they are going to look for any boldface words, words in italics, familiar words, numbers, or any other parts of the text that stand out to them. Ask students to highlight these features. Explain that they will "Stop and Think" about these features and decide if they can explain them, if they find them interesting, or if they have a question about them.

   - **Differentiation:** Draw a line between each section to show students when they should stop and think.

7. You might model this by placing a star beside the word "energy" from the sentence, "Energy radiates outward from the sun every day." Explain that you recognize this word from a science lesson and can explain what it means.

8. Have students continue to skim the text in this manner, placing their sticky notes as they go.

9. After finishing the first section, ask students where they placed their sticky notes.

10. Explain that they will write about the parts of the text they flagged. First, model writing the section title, Producers, at the top of the page.

11. Model how to remove the sticky notes from the text, one at a time, and transfer them below the Producers heading. As you transfer each sticky note, write the information that you flagged next to it. Conclude the process by reviewing your notes.

Producers and Consumers *(cont.)*

12. Tell students to continue the stop and think process with the other two sections of the text. Explain that they should use the additional sticky notes and continue the same process as they read the two sections. They can also continue the stop and think process by writing annotations in the margins of the text.
    - **Differentiation:** For students who complete the task early or need an additional challenge, encourage them to research any unanswered questions they flagged in the text.

13. This activity may run over several Lesson Input pages.

Assessment

- On the Student Output page, have students use their notes to write or draw summaries about the topic. Have students circle any questions that were not answered in the text. Have them include vocabulary words and statements that explain how this strategy helps them understand the content.

During Reading Procedure

Strategy: Peer Partner Review

1. Read the text aloud with students. Review vocabulary words related to producers and consumers. Tell students to highlight the important vocabulary words as you read, including: *producers*, *consumers*, *cycle*, *energy*, *nutrients*, *consumption*, *herbivores*, *carnivores*, *prey*, *scavengers*, and *omnivores*.

2. Distribute copies of *Producers and Consumers Peer Partner Review* (page 95) to students. Encourage them to review the questions for a minute or two and consider which questions they know they can answer. Explain that they will write answers on their classmates' activity sheets.

3. Set a timer for 10–15 minutes. Ask students to move around the room looking for peer partners. Have them swap papers with partners to answer questions on each other's papers. Tell students that they will need to verbally explain their answers to their partners after they write them.
    - **Differentiation:** For English language learners, provide sentence frames on the board that they can use to ask their partners questions. You can also create a bank of academic vocabulary words related to the questions on the review page for students to reference.

4. Be sure to set clear procedures and expectations before you begin:
    - Only answer one question on each partner's paper.
    - Sign your name next to each question you answer. This will help you keep track of which partners you have already worked with.
    - If you cannot answer a question, tell your classmate that he or she should look for another partner.
    - Always be respectful, and never make fun of a classmate who cannot answer a question.
    - After you have written your answer, explain how you found your answer and/or how you know your answer is correct.

Producers and Consumers (cont.)

5. Tell students to stop finding partners when they have just one question left.

6. Have students complete the last question independently at their own desks.

7. Tell students to cut out and glue *Producers and Consumers Peer Partner Review* onto a new Lesson Input page.

Assessment

• Ask students to review the question and answer matches that were completed on their activity sheets. Tell them to choose three of the question/answer responses and explain them on the Student Output page. You may choose to model this for students.

After Reading Procedure

Strategy: Reading–Review Web

1. Distribute two 8.5" x 11" sheets of colored paper and two sticky notes to each student. Have students fold their papers horizontally, and then fold them in half vertically. When opened, each paper should have four equal sections. Have students prepare one page for *Producers* and one page for *Consumers*.
   • In place of using separate colored paper, you may choose to distribute two copies of *Producers and Consumers Reading-Review Web* (page 96) to each student.

2. Have students write the first main idea, *Producers*, on one sticky note. Have them place it in middle of the reading-review web where the two lines/folds intersect.

3. Tell students to write the second main idea, *Consumers*, on the other sticky note and place it in the middle of the second copy of the web. Then, ask students to label each of the four sections *Supporting Detail*.

4. Explain that students should review the sections of the text and consider the images they created in their minds for producers and consumers. They should then draw or write about those images in the four *Supporting Detail* boxes on the correct reading-review web. The drawings or explanations should represent details that support each of the main ideas.
   • **Differentiation:** Challenge above-level learners to list one or two details from the text that do not specifically support the main idea but are interesting or informative.

5. Once students have completed their review webs, have them meet with partners to discuss the supporting details for the text, *Producers and Consumers*.

6. After talking with their partners, have students to make any revisions needed on their review webs to make the webs more detailed. Then, have students fold their papers over the horizontal fold again and glue them onto the next Lesson Input page.

7. Have students turn to the next Lesson Input page and attach the text, *Producers and Consumers*. Refer to pages 158–159 for options on how to attach the text.

Assessment

• Encourage students to consider how visualizing the text while they read helps them draw images to represent the main idea and supporting details. On the Student Output page, have students write what they learned about producers and consumers.

Producers and Consumers

Producers

In the nutrient cycle, producers take basic, nonliving substances. They use them to make what they need to grow and live. They make nutrients for themselves. In other words, they make their own food. To do that, they need the sun's energy.

Energy radiates outward from the sun every day. Earth receives some of this energy. It makes life on Earth possible. The energy warms the ground. It also warms oceans and lakes. Plants get this energy and use it to help them live. They use this energy to grow. They use it to make their stems and trunks, branches and leaves, and flowers and fruit. They also make their own fuel that powers all this growing. Since plants produce, or make, their own fuel, they are called *producers*. They make their fuel using energy from the sun.

Getting Energy

Animals can't use energy straight from the sun like plants can. They can't make the basic materials their bodies need. They don't use the sun's energy to power what their bodies need to do—breathe, move, and release waste.

Plants store energy in their parts. They also have nutrients. Many animals must eat plants to stay alive. They use plant materials for growing and taking care of their own bodies. This process of eating plants for their nutrients is called *consumption*. The animals are consumers. They consume their nutrients. All animals are consumers, including humans. Animals need nutrients to grow and keep their body tissues healthy.

Plants are producers.

Producers and Consumers (cont.)

Types of Consumers

One way animals get their nutrients is by eating different parts of plants. These animals are called *herbivores*. Herbivores may eat roots, stems, leaves, fruits, flowers, nectar, or seeds. Every animal has its preferences. Some eat the entire plant!

The other way for animals to get nutrients is by eating other animals. These animals are called *carnivores*. They are meat eaters. These animals mainly hunt and kill their prey. But some carnivores eat prey that has been killed by other animals or that dies naturally. These animals are scavengers.

Animals are consumers.

Many animals actually use both ways to get their nutrients. They eat plants, and they eat other animals. These animals are called *omnivores*. Humans are animals. Which type of consumer are we? We eat plants, such as carrots, peas, broccoli, and corn. We can also eat many kinds of meats, such as chicken, fish, pork, and beef. Since we eat plants and animals, we are omnivores. Other omnivores include bears, pigs, dogs, foxes, and badgers.

Name: _____ Date:_____

Producers and Consumers Peer Partner Review

Directions: Trade papers with a partner. Answer one question on their paper, and write your name at the bottom of the square where you wrote your answer. Do this again with other partners. Leave one question to answer yourself.

1. Give an example of a producer.	**2.** Explain why animals are not producers.	**3.** Where do plants store their energy?
4. What is the process of eating plants for their nutrients called?	**5.** Name the two ways animals get their nutrients.	**6.** Which type of consumers are humans?
7. What are animals that eat plants called?	**8.** What are animals that eat other animals called?	**9.** What are animals that eat both plants and animals called?

Name: _____ Date: _____

Producers and Consumers Reading-Review Web

Directions: Review the sections of the text. As you read, create images in your mind about the main idea. Then, draw or write details that support the main idea.

Supporting Detail

Supporting Detail

| Producers and Consumers |

Supporting Detail

Supporting Detail

Pocahontas

Standards

➠ **Social Studies**

Understands family life now and in the past, and family life in various places long ago.

➠ **Reading**

Interpret words and phrases as they are used in a text, including determining technical, connotative, and figurative meanings, and analyze how specific word choices shape meaning or tone.

➠ **Writing**

Write informative/explanatory texts to examine and convey complex ideas and information clearly and accurately through the effective selection, organization, and analysis of content.

Materials

- copies of *Pocahontas* (pages 102–103)

- copies of *Pocahontas Skim and Post It* (page 104) (optional)

- copies of *Pocahontas Four-Flap Vocabulary Book* (page 105) (optional)

- copies of *Pocahontas Inner/Outer Notes* (page 106) (optional)

- uncoated paper plates (1 per student)

- sticky notes (several per student)

- markers, scissors, and glue (or stapler)

- each student's interactive notebook

Graphic Organizer Examples

Before Reading— Skim and Post It

During Reading— Four-Flap Vocabulary Book

After Reading— Inner/Outer Notes

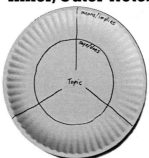

Pocahontas (cont.)

Before Reading Procedure

Strategy: Skim and Post It

1. Distribute copies of *Pocahontas* (pages 102–103) to students. Review what the term *skim* means when previewing the text, and point out the title, subheading, boldfaced words, graphics, and text structure.

2. Tell students to turn to the next Lesson Input page. Ask students to write the words *Skim* and *Post It* at the top of their pages. Below this, students should write the title of the text, *Pocahontas*.

3. Distribute five sticky notes to each student. Explain that as they skim the text, they should write the subheadings and other text features on the sticky notes.

4. You can model this by skimming some of the text together. Stop at the first subheading, and write it on a sticky note. Then, have students skim the remainder of the text, explaining that they should record any other subheadings as well as the illustrations in the text.

5. When students have finished, they should have written the following on the sticky notes:
   - Who Was Pocahontas?
   - Pocahontas Kidnapped!
   - illustration of Pocahontas
   - Life as a Captive
   - illustration of Pocahontas

6. Tell students to place the sticky notes vertically down the left margin of the Lesson Input page.
   - In place of creating this directly in the notebooks, you may choose to distribute copies of *Pocahontas Skim and Post It* (page 104) to students. Once students have completed the graphic organizers, have them cut them out and glue them onto the Lesson Input page of their interactive notebooks.

7. Once the sticky notes are in place, students should add two bullets to the right of each sticky note. The first bullet should begin with the sentence stem *I know…* and the second bullet should read *I wonder….*

8. Have students look at the sticky notes and determine their prior knowledge. If they know anything about the subheading or illustration, they should write what they know next to the *I know…* bullet. If they have a question, they should write it next to the *I wonder…* bullet.
   - **Differentiation:** To incorporate a more visual and tactile element to this activity, print extra copies of the text. Have students cut out the subheadings (or other text features) and glue them in their interactive notebooks. They should then write what they know as well as one question they have about the text features.

9. Tell students to meet with partners and discuss what they already know and the questions they have.

Assessment

- After completing this activity, tell students to summarize what they already know about Pocahontas on the Student Output page.

Pocahontas (cont.)

During Reading Procedure

Strategy: Four-Flap Vocabulary Book

1. Write the following words on the board: *colony*, *settlers*, *ransom*, and *captive*. Read the words aloud. Explain that students will read about and complete a vocabulary activity with these four vocabulary words.

2. Ask students to turn to the next Lesson Input page. Tell them to fold the edge of the page over to the center of the notebook and crease the fold. Check that each student has two columns in his or her notebook.

3. Have students unfold their pages to their full size. Students should then make three cuts beginning on the outer edge and stopping at the center fold. This will divide the outer column into fourths. Students may need support to cut the column into roughly equal fourths. Monitor students to ensure that they do not cut past the center fold.
   - In place of creating this directly in the notebooks, you may choose to distribute copies of *Pocahontas Four-Flap Vocabulary Book* (page 105) to students. Have them follow the same instructions below. At the end of the activity, have students glue their graphic organizers onto the Lesson Input page. If needed, students can fold down and glue only one section of their graphic organizers for a better fit.

4. Ask students to fold the page back over to the center fold to create a four-flap vocabulary book. With the flaps still folded over, have students label the top flap *colony*, the second flap *settlers*, the third flap *ransom*, and the fourth flap *captive*.

5. Have students read the text and underline, highlight, or circle each of the vocabulary words as they come to them.

6. Reread the text as a class, or have students reread the text independently. Students should focus on the four vocabulary words that they annotated in Step 5. Tell students to pay attention to the context surrounding each word and use the description in the text to create a definition for each word. You may need to model this initially.

7. Tell students to write each definition behind the correct flap. Have them follow the same process for all four words. After students have written their definitions, they can draw illustrations or examples that describe each vocabulary word on the remaining space behind the flaps.
   - **Differentiation:** Work with a small group of below-level learners to complete the definitions. Model how to look at the context around the word. Show them additional strategies, such as jotting down the definition in the margin as practice before writing it behind the flap. Or, alternatively, provide sentence stems to help students write definitions.

8. Tell students to work with partners to review the new vocabulary by using the four flaps to quiz each other.

Pocahontas (cont.)

Assessment

- Assess students by making observations as they work in partners or groups to quiz one another.

- On the Student Output page, ask students to use the vocabulary words in short paragraphs that describe what they learned about Pocahontas. Explain that their paragraphs should combine what they know about Pocahontas in a few concise sentences.

After Reading Procedure

Strategy: Inner/Outer Notes

1. Distribute a paper plate and a small sticky note to each student. Ask students to draw a straight line up from the center of the paper plate to the outer edge. Have them rotate the plate about one-third rotation to the right. Have them draw another straight line from the center of the plate to the outer edge. Finally, rotate the plate another one-third rotation and draw a third line from the center of the plate to the edge. This will divide the plate into three sections.

2. Have each student place the sticky note in the center of the paper plate and write *Pocahontas* on it. Then, ask students to draw a circle just inside the rough edge of the paper plate. This will create an inner circle and an outer circle. Finally, have students label the inner circle *Says/Does* and the outer circle *Means/Implies*. Explain the meaning of the word *implies*, if necessary.
   - In place of creating this on paper plates, you may choose to distribute copies of *Pocahontas Inner/Outer Notes* (page 106) to students. Have them follow the same instructions listed below. Once finished, tell students to turn to the next Lesson Input page and glue their graphic organizers.

3. Tell students they are going to read the *Pocahontas* text one more time. Explain that they will use the graphic organizer to take notes about each section as they read. Model how to record a few key ideas from the Who Was Pocahontas? section in one of the inner circles. For example, in the inner circle you might write, *Pocahontas saw British settlers arrive on large ships.*

4. Model using a think-aloud process to consider what this idea means or implies, and record your ideas in the outer circle. For example, *The American Indians thought the white settlers were different from them.*

Pocahontas (cont.)

5. Continue reading as a class or encourage students to finish reading independently. Model the process as much as needed. Each section of the plate should refer to one of the sections of the text. Each section of the plate should be completed when students are finished reading.
   - **Differentiation:** Provide students who may need additional support with slips of paper containing prewritten or pre-typed text that belongs in the inner and outer circles. Explain that they must place and glue each slip in the correct *Says/Does* or *Means/Implies* section.

6. Place students into pairs, and have them share their graphic organizers. As students are talking about their inner/outer notes, encourage them to explain their reasoning.

7. Ask students to fold their paper plates in half and glue one half onto the next Lesson Input page.

8. On the next Student Output page, have students use the information they learned from the text to explain how Pocahontas changed when she became a captive.

9. Have students turn to the next Lesson Input page and attach the text, *Pocahontas*. Refer to pages 158–159 for options on how to attach the text.

Assessment

- On the Student Output page, have students write short summary paragraphs about Pocahontas based on the information listed in their inner/outer notes. They should conclude with how Pocahontas paved the way for relationships between settlers and American Indians.

Pocahontas

Who Was Pocahontas?

Around 1595, an American Indian girl was born. Her name was Matoaka. This means "Little Snow Feather." Her father, the chief Powhatan, decided to call her Pocahontas. This means "Playful One." She had tons of energy and enjoyed playing outdoors. Her family lived in the Chesapeake Bay region. She grew up eating oysters and fish. The forest where she lived was home to deer, beavers, and wild turkeys.

Pocahontas first saw British settlers in 1607. The American Indians called the settlers "white" men because of their pale skin. Pocahontas loved to listen to stories about the white men. The white men came on large ships. They lived in a colony called Fort James. The fort was named after King James I of England. Later, the fort's name was changed to Jamestown.

The American Indians secretly watched the settlers. They hid in tall grass around the fort. The settlers looked strange to them. The white men had more hair than they did. And the white settlers wore funny-looking clothes. Everything about them seemed odd.

Pocahontas Kidnapped!

By 1613, the British and the American Indians were no longer getting along. Captain Samuel Argall decided to kidnap Pocahontas. He thought kidnapping the chief's daughter would make him want to work with the settlers. Argall convinced someone to trick Pocahontas. She came onto his ship. The captain wanted a ransom from Chief Powhatan. He wanted British prisoners set free. And he wanted the American Indians to give up their guns.

Pocahontas *(cont.)*

Argall wanted the American Indians to agree. Then Pocahontas could return home. Chief Powhatan only sent back some of the prisoners. The guns he returned were broken. He asked the settlers to take care of his daughter. She remained a captive!

Life as a Captive

Captain Argall took Pocahontas. They went to a farm in Henrico, Virginia. Today, this is near Richmond, Virginia. He was afraid. He thought her tribe would attack to get her back. A reverend taught her the Christian faith. They gave her the name Rebecca.

Pocahontas had to get rid of her deerskin clothes. She learned English. She dressed, acted, and prayed like her captors.

The kidnapping of Pocahontas changed her life. She married a man named John Rolfe on April 5, 1614. There was peace once again between the American Indians and the settlers.

Pocahontas in traditional Western attire

Name: _____ Date:_____

Pocahontas Skim and Post It

Directions: Write something you know and something you wonder for each section of the text.

Who Was Pocahontas?	I know…
	I wonder…
Pocahontas Kidnapped!	I know…
	I wonder…
Life as a Captive	I know…
	I wonder…

51733—Interactive Notetaking for Content-Area Literacy   © Shell Education

Pocahontas Four-Flap Vocabulary Book

Directions: Cut out the graphic organizer. Fold it in half along the vertical line. Then, cut along the three horizontal lines. Be sure not to cut past the fold. Fold the flaps over.

Pocahontas Inner/Outer Notes

Directions: Record key ideas from the text in the inner circle. Write what each idea means or implies in the outer circle.

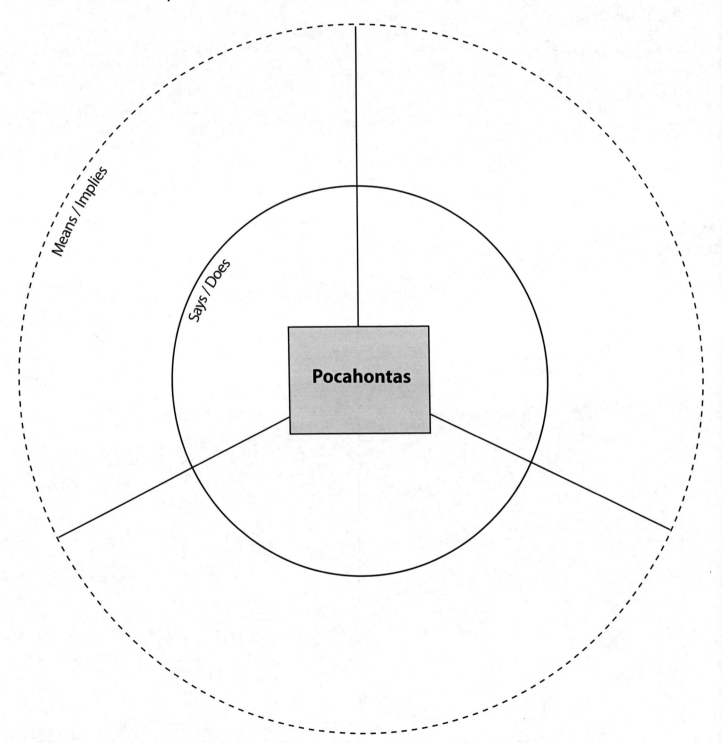

The American Government

Standards

→ **Social Studies**

Understands how democratic values came to be, and how they have been exemplified by people, events, and symbols.

→ **Reading**

Integrate and evaluate content presented in diverse media and formats, including visually and quantitatively, as well as in words.

→ **Writing**

Develop and strengthen writing as needed by planning, revising, editing, rewriting, or trying a new approach.

Materials

- copies of *The American Government* (pages 111–112)

- copies of *Government Words* (page 113) (optional)

- copies of *Government Three-Sides Notetaking* (page 114)

- copies of *Government Think-Pair-Square-Share* (page 115)

- markers, scissors, and glue (or stapler)

- each student's interactive notebook

Graphic Organizer Examples

Before Reading— Possible Sentences

During Reading— Three-Sides Notetaking

After Reading— Think-Pair-Square-Share

The American Government (cont.)

Before Reading Procedure

Strategy: Possible Sentences

1. Display the following vocabulary words on the board: *legislative branch*, *House of Representatives*, *Senate*, *Congress*, *representatives*, *executive branch*, *president*, *veto*, *Supreme Court*, *judicial branch*, *ruling*, and *justices*.
   - **Differentiation:** Preview the meanings of the vocabulary words with below-level learners. Pair vocabulary words ahead of time. Encourage students to draw pictures or write short phrases if they are not yet ready to write sentences.

2. Ask students to pair words that might be related to one another. You may need to model how to make a pair. For example, students could pair *executive branch* and *president*. Have them write the paired words on the next Lesson Input page.

3. Tell students to think about the words they paired and pay attention to what the words have in common. Ask students to write sentences using their word pairs. Explain that their sentences should be ones they expect to see in the text.
   - **Differentiation:** Above-level learners can write multiple sentences using various forms of the words and more complex sentences structures.
   - In place of creating this directly in the notebooks, you may choose to distribute copies of *Government Words* (page 113) to students. Have students cut out the cards and use them to preview the vocabulary words or pair the words.

4. Distribute copies of *The American Government* (pages 111–112) to students. Have them skim the text and compare their sentences with the sentences in the text. Encourage students to make their sentences more accurate on the Lesson Input page.

Assessment

- Have students examine their sentences for accuracy. Have students explain how to edit and revise sentences. On the Student Output page, students should write their revised sentences independently using the new knowledge and understanding of the vocabulary words.

During Reading Procedure

Strategy: Three-Sides Notetaking

1. Distribute copies of *Government Three-Sides Notetaking* (page 114) to students. Have them cut along the outer edge of the square.

2. Draw students' attention to the four triangles that make up the square. Explain that they will use the top, bottom, and right triangles for notetaking. The triangle labeled *glue* should not be written on.

3. Tell students to refer to the text, *The American Government* (pages 111–112). Explain that they will be using a notetaking strategy to help them organize their thoughts as they read.
   - **Differentiation:** Review difficult vocabulary words from the text with students. Ask students to say the words with you, and discuss the meanings of the words with students.

The American Government (cont.)

4. Explain that as students read, they should take notes in the appropriate sections of the template. Depending on students' ability levels, you may choose to model this. It is likely that students may need to read the text several times to reflect on the information in each section.
   - **Differentiation:** Provide a word bank for each section for students to refer during the notetaking strategy.

5. After students have completed their notes, have them cut along the dashed lines. Monitor to ensure that they stop in the center of the square and do not cut on the solid line beyond the cut line.

6. Have students make folds on the solid lines. Students should then put small amounts of glue on the triangle labeled *glue*. Tell students to move the bottom triangle up and over the glue section. The bottom triangle should overlap and cover the glue section. Then, students can press down lightly to adhere the glue. Students should now have three-dimensional notes pages.

7. Have students glue the triangular prism onto the next Lesson Input page. They should glue only the bottom section of the triangle to the notebook. Additionally, tell students to title the page, *The American Government*. Have students fold the triangular shapes so they lay flat.

Assessment

- On the Student Output page, each student should write a short summary paragraph for each of the branches of the government. Each of the summaries should include a main idea and details describing that particular branch. Tell students to include examples from their notes.

After Reading Procedure

Strategy: Think-Pair-Square-Share

1. Distribute copies of *Government Think-Pair-Square-Share* (page 115) to students. Put the following scenario and question on the board: *The checks and balances system is used to keep each branch from getting too powerful. Do you think this is important? What might happen if this system did not exist?*

2. Ask students to think about the question. Have students record their answers in the *Think* box on the activity sheet.
   - **Differentiation:** If necessary, create a word bank of academic vocabulary related to the questions to help students write their responses.

3. Tell students to share their answers with the person next to them. Pairs of students should collaborate to find the best answer to share with other classmates and an explanation of why it is the best. Then, have each pair write their answer and explanation in the *Pair* box on the activity sheet.

4. Have students share their answers in groups of four or more, depending on class size. Have each pair share their answers with the group. Then, each group should decide which answer they think is best as well as an explanation of their reasoning. Once an answer has been agreed upon, students should write their group's answer and the justification in the *Square* box on the activity sheet.

The American Government (cont.)

5. Ask students to share their group choices and reasoning with the class. Have each student then write the best answer he or she heard along with an explanation defending his or her choice in the *Share* box on the activity sheet.

6. Have students fold their activity sheets into quarters. Tell them to glue the bottom-right quarter of their completed *Government Think-Pair-Square-Share* activity sheets onto an empty Lesson Input page.

7. On the Student Output page, have students write summaries of their discussions. Tell students to include their final answer and why they chose it.

8. Have students turn to the next Lesson Input page and attach the text, *The American Government*. Refer to pages 158–159 for options on how to attach the text.

Assessment

- Assess students on the conversations they shared in their groups by reviewing their summaries. Look for academic vocabulary appropriate to the text, and evaluate students' reasoning for why they believe their answers are best.

The American Government

The Legislative Branch

The legislative branch is made up of two groups. One group is the House of Representatives, or simply the House. The other group is the Senate. Together, they are known as Congress. Congress is made up of leaders from each state. They make the laws.

The House is much larger than the Senate. Each state sends representatives to the House. Larger states send more people. Smaller states send fewer people. This means that bigger states have more representation in the House.

Like the House, the Senate is made up of representatives from each state. But the Senate only has two members from each state. So, each state has the same power in the Senate.

The Executive Branch

The president leads the executive branch. He or she enforces laws. This is a big job. About four million people work for this branch! The president makes sure the country runs smoothly. He or she must follow the rules in the U.S. Constitution. For example, the president cannot pass a new law alone. First, Congress has to agree that it should be a law. Then, it can be passed. This is a law in the Constitution.

Presidents represent the country in world matters. This means that they travel a lot! They tour the world to meet with other leaders. They try to keep the peace. They make plans for the future.

The American Government (cont.)

The president works closely with Congress. Congress passes bills. Each bill then goes to the president. He or she may sign the bill. This makes the bill a law. The president can also send the bill back to Congress to be changed. Or the president may veto the bill. A *veto* means the bill is rejected. This keeps Congress from being too powerful. It is part of the checks-and-balances system.

The Judicial Branch

The Supreme Court leads the judicial branch. It is the highest court in the country. It is in charge of all the courts. The Supreme Court hears the biggest cases in America. It listens to people who do not agree on something. Then, it makes a decision about what the law means. This is called a *ruling*. All courts must follow what the Supreme Court says. Its rulings become the law.

The Supreme Court tries to treat all people fairly. The Supreme Court judges are called *justices*. They choose about 100 cases to hear each year. They make rulings based on the U.S. Constitution.

The Supreme Court justices work hard to protect people's rights. They look at laws to make sure they are fair. It is the job of the Supreme Court to say how the law works. If they think a law goes against the U.S. Constitution or is unfair, it is thrown out. They have the final say on the law. Only an amendment to the U.S. Constitution can change a ruling made by the Supreme Court. An amendment is a change to the U.S. Constitution.

Government Words

Directions: Cut apart the vocabulary words.

legislative branch	House of Representatives	Senate
Congress	representatives	executive branch
president	veto	Supreme Court
judicial branch	ruling	justices

Name: _____ Date: _____

Government Three-Sides Notetaking

Directions: Cut along the outer edges of the square. Record notes about each branch of government under the correct flap. Then, cut along the dashed line. Do not cut on the solid lines.

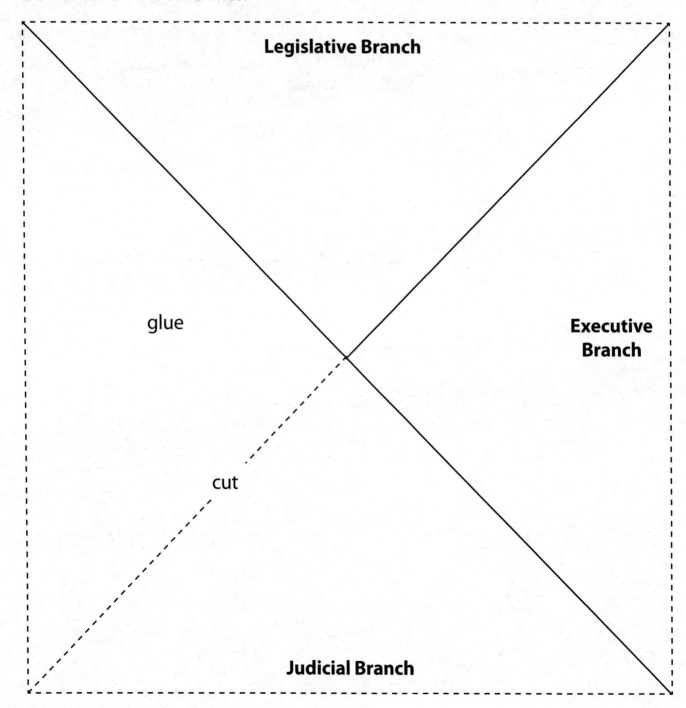

Legislative Branch

glue

Executive Branch

cut

Judicial Branch

Government Think-Pair-Square-Share

Directions: Complete the table with notes based on your discussions and the text.

Think 	Pair
Think of your answer. Write or draw your answer.	Talk with your partner. Write or draw your answer.
Square	**Share**
Meet with your group. Write or draw the best answer.	Listen to the groups. Decide on the best answer. Write or draw this answer.

Pioneer Trails

Standards

➠ **Social Studies**

Understands the history of a local community and how communities in North America varied long ago.

➠ **Reading**

Read closely to determine what the text says explicitly and to make logical inferences from it; cite specific textual evidence when writing or speaking to support conclusions drawn from the text.

➠ **Writing**

Conduct short as well as more sustained research projects based on focused questions, demonstrating understanding of the subject under investigation.

Materials

- copies of *Pioneer Trails* (pages 121–122)
- copies of *Pioneer Trails Analyzing a Photograph* (page 123)
- copies of *Pioneer Trails Venn Diagram* (page 124) (optional)
- copies of *Pioneer Trails Fact or Fib* (page 125) (optional)
- sticky notes (several per student)
- index cards (3–5 per student)
- 10-inch sealed envelope (1 per 2 students)
- markers, scissors, and glue (or stapler)
- each student's interactive notebook

Graphic Organizer Examples

Before Reading— Analyzing a Photograph

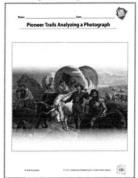

During Reading— Stop and Think

After Reading— Fact or Fib

Pioneer Trails (cont.)

Before Reading Procedure

Strategy: Analyzing a Photograph

1. Distribute copies of *Pioneer Trails Analyzing a Photograph* (page 123) to students. Ask them to develop ideas about what they think is happening. Have students share some of their thoughts, and record students' ideas on the board.

2. Refer to the text, *Pioneer Trails* (pages 121–122), and provide students with background information on the picture.

3. Have students cut out the photographs around the cut line. Then, have each student fold the frame above the photograph under to make a small flap. Tell students to glue that flap onto the top of the next Lesson Input page so the photograph will face up on the top half of the page.

4. Have each student draw a three-column chart in the space under the photograph. Have them label the first column *People*, the second column *Objects*, and the third column *Activity*.

5. Encourage students to take a close look at the image. Demonstrate how to analyze the picture by leading a think aloud, modeling how to observe and take notes about the people, objects, and activity in the picture. Tell students to continue to write observations in the correct columns.

6. Provide time for students to complete their own observations. Then, have students find partners and discuss their three-column charts. Encourage students to add items to their charts that their partners observed that they did not previously include.

7. Explain that they are going to compare and contrast the jobs people had on the Oregon Trail to the jobs people have today. Ask students to draw Venn diagrams on the Student Output page. Label the left circle *Jobs on the Oregon Trail*, the right circle *Jobs Today*, and the middle overlap *Both*. Have students think about the extreme hardships the pioneers encountered while on the Oregon Trail. Then, help students think about how there are tools today that make jobs less cumbersome in the modern world.
   - **Differentiation:** Scaffold the Venn diagram by changing the number of expected responses for various students.
   - In place of creating this directly in the notebooks, you may choose to distribute copies of *Pioneer Trails Venn Diagram* (page 124) to students. Have them complete the diagrams and then cut and glue them onto their Student Output pages.

Assessment

- Ask students to think about what life would have been like on the Oregon Trail. Have them write short journal entries titled, *A Day on the Oregon Trail*. They should include obstacles encountered during the day and how they would deal with them. Encourage students to visualize themselves in the photograph for help.

During Reading Procedure

Strategy: Stop and Think

1. Distribute nine sticky notes to each student. If possible, provide students with three different colors.

Pioneer Trails (cont.)

2. Distribute copies of *Pioneer Trails* to students. Read the text together, explaining that this is a nonfiction article. Then, explain that the text is broken into three sections: Traveling the Oregon Trail, Life on the Oregon Trail, and Searching for Gold. Read the sections in chunks. If possible, project the text on the board with the sections numbered so students can refer to it as they read.
   - **Differentiation:** Draw lines between each section to show students when they should stop and think.

3. Tell students to turn to the next Lesson Input page and title it *Stop and Think*. Directly under the strategy title, have students write the text title, "Pioneer Trails."

4. Ask students to spread out the sticky notes on their desks. Have them write exclamation points on three sticky notes, stars on three, and question marks on three. Explain what each symbol means.

   ❗ I find this interesting.

   ✳ I can explain this.

   ❓ I have a question about this.

5. Begin with the Traveling the Oregon Trail section of the text. Read the section together, and discuss the process of placing sticky notes beside sentences. For example, you might place the exclamation point beside the sentence, "They needed ten horses, mules, or oxen to pull eaach wagon." Explain that you find this interesting because you did not realize the wagons were so heavy. Have students underline the sentences they find interesting and place the exclamation points beside them.

6. After finishing the first section, provide students time to share where they placed their sticky notes.

7. Tell students to write about the parts of the text that they flagged. First, model writing the section title, Traveling the Oregon Trail, at the top of the page.

8. Model how to remove each sticky note from the text and transfer it to the notes page below the Traveling the Oregon Trail heading. As you remove each sticky note, write the information that you flagged in the right section of the notes page. Conclude by reviewing your notes.

9. Tell students to continue the stop and think process with the other two sections of the text. Explain that they should use the additional sticky notes and continue the same process as they reread the two sections.
   - **Differentiation:** For students who complete the task early or need an additional challenge, encourage them to research any unanswered questions they flagged in the text.

10. This activity may run over several Lesson Input pages.

Assessment

- On the Student Output page, have students use their notes to write or draw summaries about the topic. Have students circle any questions that were not answered in the text. Have them include vocabulary words and statements that explain how this strategy helps them understand the content.

Pioneer Trails (cont.)

After Reading Procedure

Strategy: Fact or Fib

1. After students have read "Pioneer Trails," place them into heterogeneous groups of four or five. Assign a section of the text for each group to read and review.

2. Distribute index cards to students. Have each group create two to four fact cards and one fib card for their assigned section of the text. Tell students that although they will choose their facts and fibs as a group, each student will need to make his or her own copy of the group's fact and fib cards.

3. To create the fact cards, ask students to review their sections and write facts on the fronts of their index cards. Tell students to choose facts they think are most important. On the backs of their cards, have students write evidence to support the facts.

4. Model how to create a fib card that is relevant and appropriate for the content, but that is also untrue. Have students write the fibs on the fronts of their last index cards.
   - **Differentiation:** Create several example fact cards before students begin the activity using the ones provided in *Pioneer Trails Fact or Fib* (page 125). Model how to change a fact statement to a fib. Then, have students write the fibs on the backs of the cards and explain how they created the fibs from the facts.

5. Distribute one envelope to every two students. Ask each pair of students to cut it in half horizontally to create two pockets. Each student should take one half and write the title, *Pioneer Trails*, on the envelope.

6. Have students attach the envelope pocket onto the next Lesson Input page and place the fact or fib cards in their envelope pocket.

7. Explain that you will now jigsaw their groups. Place students into new groups so that each group has a student for every section of the text. The new groups will then take turns using the fact or fib cards to quiz each other. (Make sure they mix up their cards before starting so that the fib cards aren't always everyone's last card.)

8. Have students share with their group the section of text they were responsible for reviewing. Ask them to read their fact or fib statements to the rest of the group. The group will then discuss which of the statements they think are the facts and which statement is a fib. They may use the text to help them. Encourage students to take notes about the group discussion on the Student Output page.

9. Discuss how students' levels of knowledge about pioneers have increased since the beginning of the lesson.

10. Have students turn to the next Lesson Input page and attach the text, *Pioneer Trails*. Refer to pages 158–159 for options on how to attach the text.

Assessment

- On the Student Output page, ask students to write the numbers *3, 2, 1* vertically down the page. Next to *3*, have students write three facts they learned about pioneers. Next to *2*, have them write two facts they found interesting about pioneers. Next to *1*, have students write one question they have about pioneers. Provide sentence stems if needed.

Pioneer Trails

Traveling the Oregon Trail

The Oregon Trail started in Independence, Missouri. It ended at the Pacific Ocean. The pioneers loaded their wagons at the beginning of the trail. They needed ten horses, mules, or oxen to pull each wagon. The large wagons had canvas tops and were about 10 feet (3 meters) long. People had to fit most of their belongings inside their wagons.

"Oregon Fever" spread as hundreds of pioneers began the six-month journey west. The pioneers needed to make the trip when there was prairie grass for the animals to eat. They also needed to cross the mountains before winter began. So, most of the groups left Missouri by early spring.

Life on the Oregon Trail

On the trail, men had the jobs of herding livestock and hunting. Some men were scouts. They rode in front of the wagon trains. The scouts looked for problems ahead. Pioneers worried about floods or hostile American Indians. Cholera, smallpox, the flu, and other diseases killed many pioneers. The trail was dangerous. Some travelers drowned while crossing rivers or were run over by the wagons.

Along the trail, women cared for the children and cooked. Common meals included bread, beans, and bacon. Women had to wash and mend clothes as well. There were no stores on the trail for buying new clothes. Children had jobs, too. Older girls helped their mothers with chores. Older boys helped their fathers herd the livestock. Children also had to milk the cows. Young children found buffalo chips. They used the chips as fuel to light fires. They used them as toys, too! Children would play catch with them. Pioneer children also played hide-and-seek and tag. Sometimes they sang songs or read books along the trail.

Pioneer Trails (cont.)

Searching for Gold

The California Trail stretched from St. Joseph, Missouri, to San Francisco, California. The first people to travel to California were in search of good soil and a mild climate. Others hoped to start businesses.

In 1848, gold was found at Sutter's Mill in California. James Marshall found small pieces of gold in the water near the mill he was building. He and John Sutter wanted to keep this a secret. Then, a worker at Sutter's Mill used a piece of gold to buy a drink. The news spread quickly across the country.

"We're off to the mines!" shouted thousands of people as they left for California. Some of them were called "forty-niners" because they left for California in 1849. These gold seekers packed all their tools for digging in small wooden wagons. They followed trail guidebooks written by people who had traveled the California Trail before.

Many miners reached California too late to participate in the gold rush. At the beginning of the gold rush, people could easily find gold dust and nuggets in streams. But more people moved to California. Gold was not found as easily. Only the large companies with machines could reach the gold that was now found underground.

Pioneer Trails Analyzing a Photograph

Pioneer Trails Venn Diagram

Directions: Complete the Venn diagram to compare and contrast jobs on the Oregon Trail and jobs today. Write how the jobs are different in the outer circles. Write how the jobs are the same where the circles overlap.

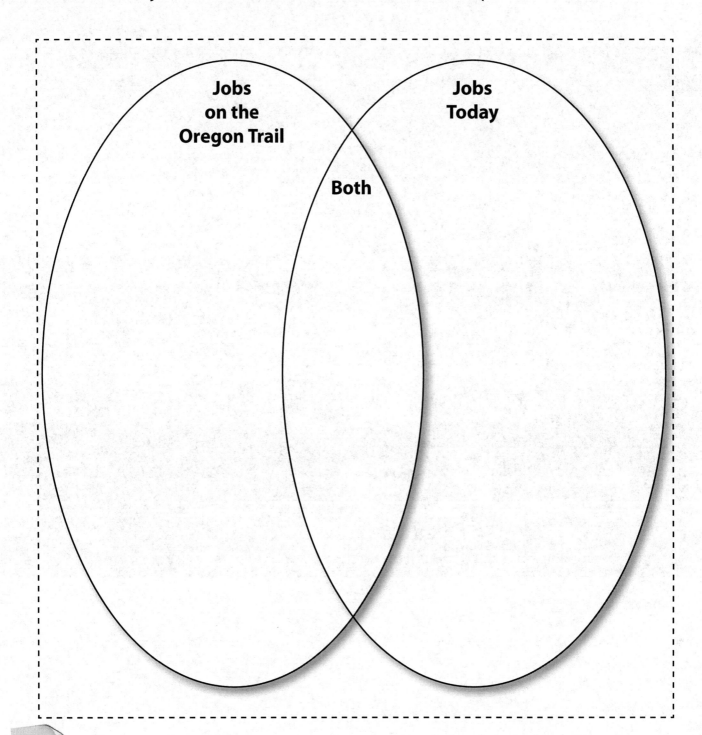

Pioneer Trails Fact or Fib

Directions: Directions: Cut each card apart. Decide which statements are facts and which are fibs.

Traveling the Oregon Trail	It began in Independence, Missouri, and it ended at the Pacific Ocean.
Life on the Oregon Trail	Cholera, smallpox, the flu, and other diseases killed many pioneers.
Life on the Oregon Trail	Meals included bread, beans, and bacon.
Searching for Gold	Gold was first found in California at Sutter's Mill.
Searching for Gold	Some of them were called "forty-niners."

Jackie Robinson

Standards

➤ Reading

Analyze how and why individuals, events, or ideas develop and interact over the course of a text.

➤ Writing

Write narratives to develop real or imagined experiences or events using effective technique, well-chosen details and well-structured event sequences.

➤ Speaking and Listening

Prepare for and participate effectively in a range of conversations and collaborations with diverse partners, building on others' ideas and expressing their own clearly and persuasively.

Materials

- copies of *Jackie Robinson* (pages 131–132)

- copies of *Jackie Robinson Preview Log* (page 133)

- copies of *Jackie Robinson Peer Partner Review* (page 134)

- copies of *Jackie Robinson Concept Map* (page 135) (optional)

- timer

- sticky notes (several per student)

- markers, scissors, and glue (or stapler)

- each student's interactive notebook

Graphic Organizer Examples

Before Reading—Preview Log

During Reading—Peer Partner Review

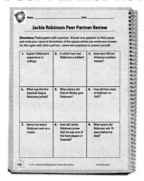

After Reading—Concept Map

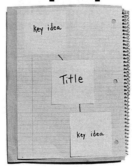

Jackie Robinson *(cont.)*

Before Reading Procedure

Strategy: Preview Log

1. Distribute copies of *Jackie Robinson* (pages 131–132) and *Jackie Robinson Preview Log* (page 133) to students. Explain that before they read the text, they will brainstorm ideas about the text using the *Jackie Robinson Preview Log* as a guide.

2. Tell students to preview the text by skimming for key vocabulary words and text features, such as subheadings, boldfaced words, captions, images, or illustrations.

3. Have students meet with partners or in small groups and discuss the talking points on their preview logs. Students should record their thoughts on their *Jackie Robinson Preview Log* activity sheets.
   - **Differentiation:** To meet the needs of the diverse learners, place students into heterogeneous groups. This will encourage all students to learn from each other and decrease the stress for below-level learners.

4. After completing their preview logs, have students share what they have written with the class. Encourage students to discuss the information using content-area and academic vocabulary related to the content they previewed.

5. Have students fold their preview logs in half vertically. Using only a small amount of glue, tell students to glue their preview logs onto the Lesson Input page.

Assessment

- Have students place three sticky notes on the Student Output page. Label the sticky notes: *Related Topics*, *Key Vocabulary*, and *Proper Nouns*. As they read the text, students may find the topic is related to other lessons. Ask students to write these on the sticky note labeled *Related Topics*. Students may also encounter additional vocabulary words and unfamiliar proper nouns. Ask students to list these words and ideas on the correct sticky notes.

During Reading Procedure

Strategy: Peer Partner Review

1. Read the text aloud with students. Review vocabulary words related to Jackie Robinson and baseball. Tell students to highlight the important vocabulary words as you read, including: *records, varsity letter, Major League Baseball, cruel, stealing bases*, and *pennants*.

2. Distribute copies of *Jackie Robinson Peer Partner Review* (page 134) to students. Encourage them to review the questions for a minute or two and consider which questions they know they can answer. Explain that they will write answers on their classmates' activity sheets.

Jackie Robinson (cont.)

3. Set a timer for 10–15 minutes. Ask students to move around the room looking for peer partners. Have them swap papers with partners to answer questions on each other's papers. Tell students that they will need to verbally explain their answers to their partners after they write them.
   - **Differentiation:** For English language learners, provide sentence frames on the board that they can use to ask their partners questions. You can also create a bank of academic vocabulary words related to the questions on the review page for students to reference.

4. Be sure to set clear procedures and expectations before you begin:
   - Only answer one question on each partner's paper.
   - Sign your name next to each question you answer. This will help you keep track of which partners you have already worked with.
   - If you cannot answer a question, tell your classmate that he or she should look for another partner.
   - Always be respectful, and never make fun of a classmate who cannot answer a question.
   - After you have written your answer, explain how you found your answer and/or how you know your answer is correct.

5. Ask students to stop finding partners when they have two questions left.

6. Have students complete the last two questions independently at their own desks.

7. Tell students to cut out and glue their completed *Jackie Robinson Peer Partner Review* onto a new Lesson Input page.

Assessment

- Ask students to review the question and answer matches that were completed on their activity sheets. Tell them to choose three of the question/answer responses and explain them on the Student Output page. You may need to model this for students.

After Reading Procedure

Strategy: Concept Map

1. Prior to the lesson, create a Concept Map on a blank sheet of paper using sticky notes. To do so, place one sticky note in the center of the paper. Label it, *Jackie Robinson*. Then, arrange 3–5 sticky notes around the center and draw lines connecting the topic sticky note to each of the surrounding notes. These outer notes will be used to record key details in the text.

2. Begin the lesson by showing students the concept map model. Explain that the purpose of a concept map is to visually represent information. Concept maps help show how individual ideas or elements connect to form a larger whole.

3. Distribute sticky notes to students. Have students create their own concept maps on the next Lesson Input page. You may want to predetermine the number of key details students should include based on what students should glean from the text. This will determine the number of outer sticky notes in the concept map model. Students should write the title, *Jackie Robinson*, at the top of the page.

Jackie Robinson (cont.)

4. After students have set up their concept maps, they should write the topic, *Jackie Robinson*, in the center sticky note of the maps. Students will follow while you demonstrate how to take notes on the map as you read.
   - In place of creating this directly in the notebooks, you may choose to distribute copies of *Jackie Robinson Concept Map* (page 135) to students. After students have completed the concept maps, have them cut them out and glue them to the Lesson Input page of their interactive notebooks.

5. Read the introduction of the text, and model how you recognize a key detail about the topic. Model writing on one of the outer sticky notes: *Robinson was born in Georgia on January 31, 1919.*

6. Have students read the first section and find another key detail about Jackie Robinson.
   - **Differentiation:** For below-level learners or English language learners, provide key vocabulary words from the text before reading. Either create a word bank, or write the words on the board.

7. Tell students to continue reading and repeating the process. Encourage them to find at least one more key detail from the first section and two more key details from the second and third sections.

8. Once you have completed reading the text and students have filled their maps with notes, have them work with partners to discuss the information they wrote on their concept maps.

9. Have students turn to the next Lesson Input page and attach the text, *Jackie Robinson*. Refer to pages 158–159 for options on how to attach the text.

Assessment

- Have students choose three key vocabulary words from the text they included in their key details sticky notes. On the Student Output page, tell students to explain what these words mean and what their relevance is to the topic of the text.

Name: _____ Date: _____

Jackie Robinson

Jackie Robinson was born in Georgia on January 31, 1919. He was good at every sport he tried.

Robinson worked hard to get into college. There, he played many sports. He broke records in basketball, football, and track. He was the first person to earn a varsity letter in four sports at his college.

Facing Unfairness

Robinson left college early. He left to join the army in World War II. Robinson saw that African American soldiers were not treated the same as white soldiers.

At that time, African Americans were not allowed to play on sports teams with white players. Major League Baseball was open to white players only. Robinson played in the Negro League. He was one of the star players.

In 1945, Robinson met Branch Rickey. Branch ran the Brooklyn Dodgers. He asked Robinson to play Major League Baseball. He told Robinson that when people were cruel, he couldn't fight back. He would have to stay calm. Robinson agreed.

When Robinson appeared on the field in 1947, many fans and players booed. They called him bad names. But Robinson trained hard and played his best.

Jackie Robinson (cont.)

Yet some of the other players treated Robinson badly. They hit him and swore at him. A few tried to kick him with spiked shoes! Robinson never fought back. He didn't call people bad names. He wanted to prove that African American and white players could play ball together.

A Great Career

Robinson played first base for the Brooklyn Dodgers. He was a great hitter. He was good at stealing bases, too. Robinson was the first person to win the Rookie-of-the-Year award. It is given to the best new player.

Robinson was one of the best players in baseball. He had a lifetime batting average of .311. He won the Most-Valuable-Player award. He led the Brooklyn Dodgers to six pennants. These were big wins. The team even won the World Series!

Robinson proved that he deserved to be in the Major League. Robinson made it into the Baseball Hall of Fame in 1962. He died 10 years later.

Jackie Robinson Preview Log

Directions: Skim *Jackie Robinson*. Look for key vocabulary words and images that give an idea of what the story is about. Record your thoughts.

Jackie Robinson Preview Log
How does this topic relate to previous lessons?
Key Vocabulary
Unfamiliar Proper Nouns
What do I already know about this topic?
I think that I am going to learn about…

Jackie Robinson Peer Partner Review

Directions: Trade papers with a partner. Answer one question on their paper, and write your name at the bottom of the square where you wrote your answer. Do this again with other partners. Leave two questions to answer yourself.

1. Explain Robinson's experience in college.	**2.** In which war was Robinson a soldier?	**3.** How were African American soldiers treated?
4. What was the first baseball league Robinson joined?	**5.** What advice did Branch Rickey give Robinson?	**6.** How did fans react to Robinson in 1947?
7. Name the award Robinson won as a rookie.	**8.** How did Jackie Robinson prove that he was one of the best players in baseball?	**9.** What award did Robinson win 10 years before he died?

Jackie Robinson Concept Map

Directions: Write key details about Jackie Robinson in the boxes.

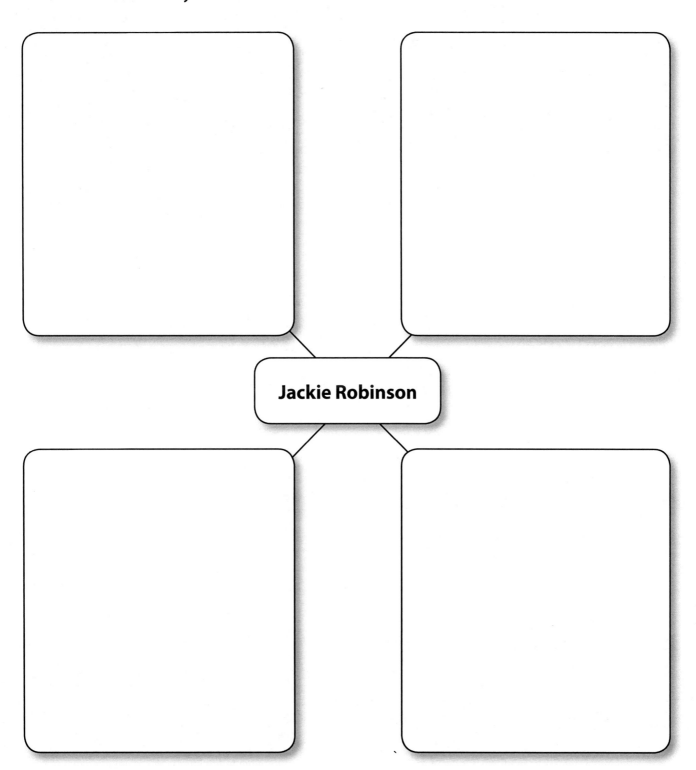

51733—Interactive Notetaking for Content-Area Literacy

Excerpt from *Anne of Green Gables*

Standards

⟫ **Reading**

Read closely to determine what the text says explicitly and to make logical inferences from it; cite specific textual evidence when writing or speaking to support conclusions drawn from the text.

⟫ **Writing**

Produce clear and coherent writing in which the development, organization, and style are appropriate to task, purpose, and audience.

⟫ **Speaking and Listening**

Prepare for and participate effectively in a range of conversations and collaborations with diverse partners, building on others' ideas and expressing their own clearly and persuasively.

Materials

* copies of *Excerpt from Anne of Green Gables* (pages 141–142)

* copies of *Anne of Green Gables Clock Partners* (page 143) (optional)

* copies of *Anne of Green Gables Three-Sides Notetaking* (page 144)

* copies of *Anne of Green Gables Reading-Review Web* (page 145) (optional)

* uncoated paper plates (1 per student)

* sticky notes (several per student)

* 8.5" x 11" sheets of colored paper (1 per student)

* markers, scissors, and glue (or stapler)

* each student's interactive notebook

Graphic Organizer Examples

Before Reading— Clock Partners

During Reading— Three-Sides Notetaking

After Reading— Reading-Review Web

Excerpt from *Anne of Green Gables* (cont.)

Before Reading Procedure

Strategy: Clock Partners

1. Distribute a paper plate and three sticky notes to each student. Have students write their names in the centers of their paper plates. Model how to label the hours of the clock (1 through 12) around the edges of their plates. Then, draw lines from the center of the plate to each of the 12 hours where students will write their names. Then, have students create their own plates following your modeled example.

   - **Differentiation:** Limit the number of hours put on the clock at one time. Start with only four hours, and then add the others a few days later.
   - In place of creating this on paper plates, you may choose to distribute copies of *Anne of Green Gables Clock Partners* (page 143) to students.

2. Have students find one classmate for each labeled hour. When they find a partner, have them write each other's names beside the same hour. For example, Kyle partners with Pedro. They both write each other's names in the 4:00 spot. Remind students that they must each find a different partner for each hour and that all their hours must be filled. Provide a few minutes for students to find partners.

   - **Differentiation:** Model how to find partners by choosing a student "partner" and acting out the process of "scheduling" a time slot. Repeat the process of writing each other's names a couple of times before encouraging students to continue on their own.

3. Once students have found their partners, have them attach their completed paper plates (or copies of completed page 143) onto an empty Lesson Input page.

4. Distribute copies of *Excerpt from Anne of Green Gables* (pages 141–142) to students. Tell them that they will meet with their 1:00 partner to preview the text. Tell students to underline the words, *Excerpt from*, and discuss what this means. Explain that they should highlight the title. Explain that *excerpt* means that only a part of the story will be discussed. Ask students to talk about whom or what the text is going to be about.

5. Have students meet with a different clock partner to skim the text. Tell students to chunk the text by paragraphs. Show students how to put brackets around each paragraph and number paragraphs sequentially.

6. Read the first paragraph as a group. Have students meet with another clock partner and reread the first paragraph. Tell students to create a question for the first paragraph. They should each write a question on a sticky note. For example, they may have noticed the phrase "girl who was sitting on a pile of shingles" while skimming the text and ask the questions, *Why would a girl be sitting alone on shingles? Was she waiting for the train all by herself?*

7. Call out another clock partner and repeat Step 6 for the remaining paragraphs as time allows. Remind students to look at the photographs as they skim the text.

8. Tell students to glue their sticky-note questions onto the next Student Output page. Then, have them share some of the questions they wrote with the rest of the class.

Excerpt from *Anne of Green Gables* (cont.)

9. As students continue to read the text more closely, they should look for answers to their questions. If they find answers to their own questions, have them jot down the answers on the Student Output page next to their sticky notes.

Assessment

• During the conversations between clock partners, listen for words such as *shingles*, *stationmaster*, *imagination*, *Nova Scotia*, and *Matthew*.

• Ask students to write any answers they found to their questions on the Student Output page. Monitor the pages to see if students are successfully answering their own questions.

During Reading Procedure

Strategy: Three-Sides Notetaking

1. Distribute copies of *Anne of Green Gables Three-Sides Notetaking* (page 144) to students. Have them cut along the outer edge of the square on the handout.

2. Draw students' attention to the four triangles that make up the square. Explain that they will use the top, bottom, and right triangles for notetaking. The triangle labeled *glue* should not be written on.

3. Tell students to refer to the text, *Excerpt from Anne of Green Gables*. Explain that they will be using a notetaking strategy to help them organize their thoughts as they read. Tell students that they will be taking notes on the personality traits of the two main characters in the text.

4. Explain that as students read, they should take notes in the appropriate sections of the template. Depending on students' ability levels, you may choose to model this. It is likely that students may need to read the text several times to reflect on the important pieces of information in each section.

   • **Differentiation:** Create a word bank of adjectives students can reference when describing the personality traits of the two main characters. If needed, students can create picture cards to help explain the different adjectives in the word bank.

5. After students have completed their notes, tell them to think about their own personality traits. They should write those traits in the right triangle labeled, *My Traits*.

6. Have students cut along the dashed lines. Monitor to ensure that they stop in the center of the square and do not cut on the solid line beyond the cut line.

7. Have students make folds on the solid lines. Students should then put small amounts of glue on the triangle labeled *glue*. Tell students to move the bottom triangle up and over the glue section. The bottom triangle should overlap and cover the glue section. Then, students can press down lightly to adhere the glue. Students should now have three-dimensional notes pages.

8. Have students glue the triangular prisms onto the next Lesson Input page. They should glue only the bottom section of the triangles to the notebooks. Additionally, tell students to title the page *Excerpt from Anne of Green Gables*. Have students fold the triangular shapes so they lay flat.

Excerpt from *Anne of Green Gables* (cont.)

Assessment

- On the Student Output page, students should write a short character analysis paragraph for each of the characters. Each of the summaries should include a main idea and details describing that particular character. Tell students that they should refer back to the notes they recorded on their graphic organizers for specific examples to include in their paragraphs.

- Challenge students to write a third character analysis about themselves.

After Reading Procedure

Strategy: Reading-Review Web

1. Distribute an 8.5" x 11" sheet of colored paper and a sticky note to each student. Have students fold their papers horizontally, and then fold them in half vertically. When opened, the papers should have four equal sections.
   - In place of using separate colored paper, you may choose to distribute copies of *Anne of Green Gables Reading-Review Web* (page 145) to students.

2. Have each students place a sticky note in the center of the folded paper and title it, *Excerpt from Anne of Green Gables*. Then, ask students to label each of the four sections, *Supporting Detail*.

3. Explain that students should reread the text and think about the important details that support *Excerpt from Anne of Green Gables*. Students should then draw or write about those details in the four *Supporting Detail* boxes. The drawings or explanations should represent details that support the main idea.

- **Differentiation:** Challenge above-level learners to list one or two examples of details from the text that do not specifically support the main idea but are interesting or informative.

4. Once students have completed their review webs, have them meet with their 12:00 partners (chosen in the Before Reading section), and discuss what they have written or drawn as the supporting details for the text, *Excerpt from Anne of Green Gables*.

5. After talking with their partners, tell students to make any revisions needed on their review webs to make the webs more detailed. Then, have students fold their papers over the horizontal fold again and glue them onto the next Lesson Input page.

6. Have students turn to the next Lesson Input page and attach the text, *Excerpt from Anne of Green Gables*. Refer to pages 158–159 for options on how to attach the text.

Assessment

- On the Student Output page, have students reflect on the text, *Excerpt from Anne of Green Gables,* and write about how Matthew handles the surprising situation he is in and how they might handle the situation themselves.

- Have students who need a challenge write questions they would have asked Anne when they saw her at the train station on the Student Output page.

Excerpt from *Anne of Green Gables*

by Lucy Maud Montgomery

When he reached Bright River there was no sign of any train. The only living creature in sight was a girl who was sitting on a pile of shingles at the extreme end. Matthew, barely noting that it was a girl, sidled past her as quickly as possible without looking at her. Had he looked he could hardly have failed to notice the tense rigidity and expectation of her attitude and expression. She was sitting there waiting for something or somebody.

Matthew encountered the stationmaster locking up the ticket office preparatory to go home for supper. He asked him if the five-thirty train would soon be along.

"The five-thirty train has been in and gone half an hour ago," answered that brisk official. "But there was a passenger dropped off for you. It was a little girl. She is sitting out there on the shingles. I asked her to go into the ladies' waiting room. She informed me gravely that she preferred to stay outside. 'There was more scope for imagination,' she said. She is a case, I should say."

"I am not expecting a girl," said Matthew blankly. "It is a boy I have come for. He should be here. Mrs. Alexander Spencer was to bring him over from Nova Scotia for me."

The stationmaster whistled.

"Guess there's some mistake," he said. "Mrs. Spencer came off the train with that girl and gave her into my charge. Said you and your sister were adopting her from an orphan asylum and that you would be along for her presently. That is all I know about it. I haven't got any more orphans concealed hereabouts."

Excerpt from *Anne of Green Gables* (cont.)

"I don't understand," said Matthew helplessly. He was wishing that Marilla was at hand to cope with the situation.

"Well, you'd better question the girl," said the stationmaster carelessly. "I dare say she will be able to explain. She's got a tongue of her own. That is certain. Maybe they were out of boys of the brand you wanted."

The stationmaster walked jauntily away, being hungry. The unfortunate Matthew was left alone to do that which was harder for him than bearding a lion in its den. He had to walk up to a girl. She was a strange girl. She was an orphan girl. He had to demand of her why she wasn't a boy. Matthew groaned in spirit as he turned about. He shuffled gently down the platform towards her.

She had been watching him ever since he had passed her. She had her eyes on him now. Matthew was not looking at her. He would not have seen what she was really like if he had been. Yet an ordinary observer would have seen a child of about eleven. She was garbed in a very short, very tight, very ugly dress of yellowish-gray wincey. She wore a faded brown sailor hat. Beneath the hat, extending down her back, were two braids of very thick, decidedly red hair. Her face was small, white, and thin, also much freckled; her mouth was large and so were her eyes, which looked green in some lights and moods and gray in others.

So far, the ordinary observer; an extraordinary observer might have seen that the chin was very pointed and pronounced; that the big eyes were full of spirit and vivacity; that the mouth was sweet-lipped and expressive; that the forehead was broad and full; in short, our discerning extraordinary observer might have concluded that no commonplace soul inhabited the body of this stray woman-child of whom shy Matthew Cuthbert was so ludicrously afraid.

Name: _____ Date: _____

Anne of Green Gables Clock Partners

Directions: Write a partner's name in each hour. You should have 12 different partners when you are finished.

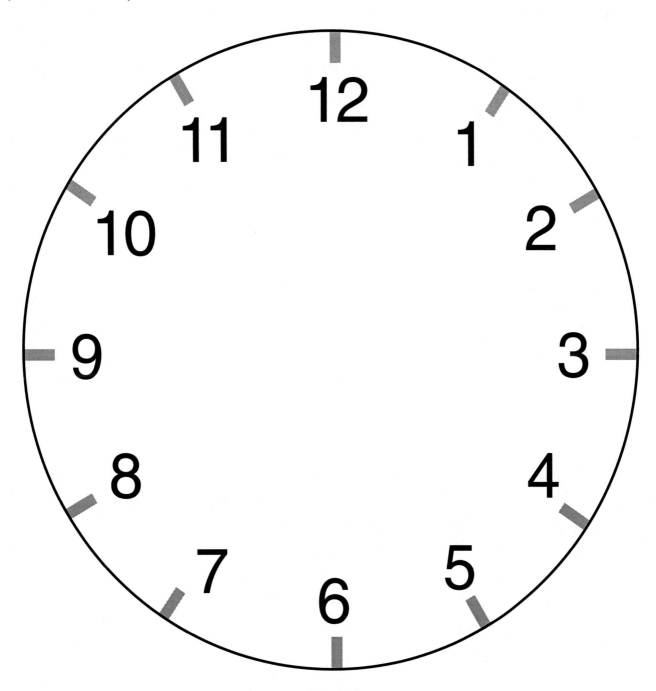

Anne of Green Gables Three-Sides Notetaking

Directions: Cut along the outer edges of the square. Record notes about each character under the correct flap. Then, cut along the dashed line. Do not cut on the solid lines.

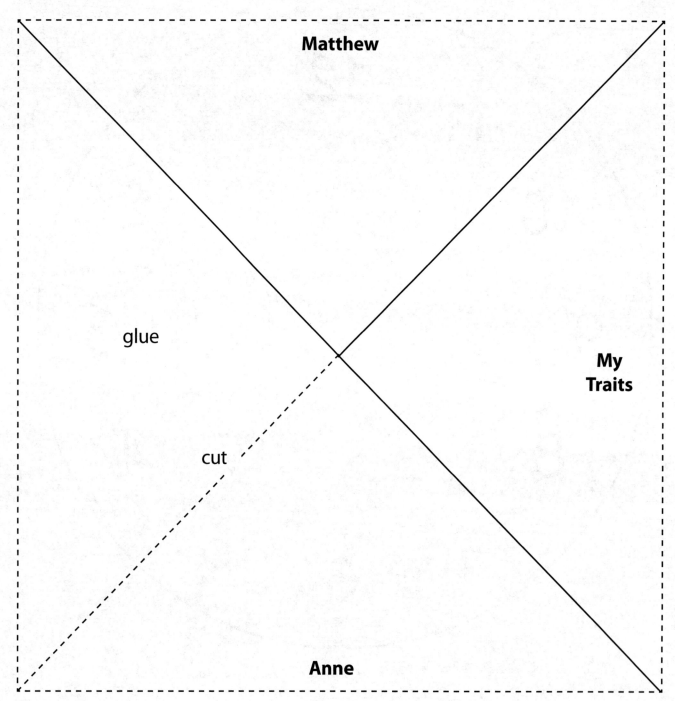

Matthew

glue

My Traits

cut

Anne

Anne of Green Gables Reading-Review Web

Directions: Review the sections of the text. As you read, create images in your mind about the main idea. Then, draw or write details that support the main idea.

Supporting Detail

Supporting Detail

Excerpt from *Anne of Green Gables*

Supporting Detail

Supporting Detail

51733—Interactive Notetaking for Content-Area Literacy